Josiah Shurtliff

EIGHTH EDITION

A STUDY GUIDE FOR PALMER/COLTON

A HISTORY
OF THE
MODERN
WORLD

Joel Colton
Duke University

McGraw-Hill, Inc.
New York   St. Louis   San Francisco   Auckland   Bogotá   Caracas
Lisbon   London   Madrid   Mexico City   Milan   Montreal   New Delhi
San Juan   Singapore   Sydney   Tokyo   Toronto

A STUDY GUIDE FOR PALMER/COLTON: A HISTORY OF THE MODERN WORLD

This book is printed on acid-free paper.

9 10 DOC/DOC 0 9 8 7 6 5 4 3 2 1 0

ISBN 0-07-040828-9

This book was set in Times Roman by Monotype Composition Company.
The editors were Nancy Blaine and Joseph F. Murphy;
the production supervisor was Annette Mayeski.
The cover was designed by Rafael Hernandez.
R. R. Donnelley & Sons Company was printer and binder.

CONTENTS

OUTLINE MAPS

INTRODUCTION

THIS NEW edition of the *Study Guide* has been prepared to accompany the eighth edition of *A History of the Modern World*. History, in one definition, is the attempt to rethink the record of our civilization. The *Study Guide*, in this edition as in earlier ones, seeks to assist students to develop for themselves a more precise knowledge of the past so that they too can share in that undertaking. Based on the premise that whatever can be repeated from memory is not history, this *Study Guide* has been designed with the express purpose of stimulating reflection and interpretation. Written with a broad range of student capabilities in mind, and including a variety of exercises, it provides students with supplementary guidance, encouragement, and study aid as well as opportunities to review their own progress.

A History of the Modern World consists of twenty-four chapters, each of which is divided into sections. Each section may be considered a smaller chapter in itself and often corresponds to a class assignment. These sections, of which there are 129 in the text, have been employed as the basic units of the *Study Guide*. This plan should have the advantage of assisting students to prepare for class assignments as well as for examinations. Although the *Study Guide* has been prepared for the one-volume edition of *A History of the Modern World*, it can be used equally effectively for either of the two volumes in the paperback edition.

For each section in the text the *Study Guide* contains Study Questions, Key Discussion Sentences, and Identifications. For each chapter there are General Essay Questions and General Discussion Passages. The General Essay Questions cover the chapter as a whole and occasionally range beyond the immediate chapter contents. In appropriate instances, Map Exercises are provided. The instructions that follow explain in greater detail the nature of these various exercises.

We hope that the *Study Guide* will continue to prove of value both to instructors and to students, and contribute an additional measure of satisfaction, interest, and stimulation to all courses in which *A History of the Modern World* is being read. The staff of the College Division of McGraw-Hill, Inc., has been unfailingly helpful in the production of the *Study Guide* and of the eighth edition of the text itself. Shirley Baron Colton has again provided various forms of valuable editorial assistance. We are especially grateful to the many readers who have used earlier editions and have offered thoughtful suggestions and comments.

JOEL COLTON

INSTRUCTIONS

Please refer to these instructions frequently as you use the *Study Guide*. They are not repeated in the pages that follow. You will find that each of the exercises described below examines the material you are studying in a different way. You will wish, therefore, to complete all of the exercises as you read each section of the text.

Study Questions

These questions are intended to help you evaluate your understanding of the most significant aspects of each section. In order to test your comprehension of what you have read, make an effort to answer each question in your own words, not in the language of the text.

Key Discussion Sentences

These sentences, taken from the text directly or with slight modification, will draw your attention to the central ideas in each section. Ask yourself whether you understand each Key Discussion Sentence and its implications. Consider each a topic sentence that might be expanded into a brief essay of one or more paragraphs. Note that these sentences are not meant to be memorized but to be analyzed and discussed.

Identifications

Identify or explain the items listed, indicating the historical significance of each and giving approximate dates wherever possible. Explain the importance of the event, book, concept, or idea in its own time and, if applicable, the reason or reasons for its continuing importance; do the same for each individual mentioned. Your ability to identify or explain these items will test your grasp of the specific information in each section and enable you to see the relationships of the details to larger themes.

Map Exercises

In most instances, you will be asked to answer questions about a specific map and the caption that accompanies it in the textbook, or to locate places mentioned in the text. In some cases, you will be asked to use an outline map in the *Study Guide* and indicate boundaries or follow other instructions. The maps and the accompanying captions in the text should be consulted frequently, as well as the maps inside the front and back covers of the text (the end papers).

General Essay Questions

These questions are intended to cover the contents of the entire chapter or at times of more than one chapter, providing an opportunity for you to review broader developments and larger themes. You may wish to prepare a sketch, rough notes, or an outline for the essay you would write in response.

General Discussion Passages

These passages, taken from the text directly or with slight modification, transcend in importance the immediate subject, suggest the nature of historical generalization, or convey implications of contemporary significance. Reflect on, discuss, and debate the meaning of these passages. The General Discussion Passages are not included in each section but appear at the end of each chapter.

Illustrations and Picture Essays

Questions on the illustrations in the text and on the more extended Picture Essays are included in the section to which they most closely relate, or at the end of the appropriate chapter.

Additional Instructions

You will find it useful to refer to the Chronological Tables and the lists of Rulers and Regimes which appear as Appendixes in the textbook. Note also that the index gives the birth and death dates for persons mentioned in the text and the pronunciation of unusual names and foreign phrases.

You will also find it helpful to refer to the Bibliography. At the end of each chapter in the Bibliography, studies in historical interpretation of individual topics are listed. The use of these books or pamphlets, either under the guidance of your instructor or on your own, will enable you to examine printed source materials, compare interpretations, deepen your understanding of the particular subject you are studying, and develop your powers of independent judgment. For more extensive readings, such as might be desired for supplementary reading or book reports, or as background for research papers, your attention is called to the annotated Bibliography as a whole, which lists and comments on several thousand volumes.

I.
THE RISE OF EUROPE
PREFACE, pp. xv–xvi
A FEW WORDS ON
GEOGRAPHY, pp. 1–7
SECTIONS 1–4, pp. 9–45

Preface and a Few Words on Geography

Study Questions

1. As you read the Preface, what do you learn about the objectives of this book? What emphasis will be given to "political decision"? How may political history be related to all other kinds of history?
2. What relationships may be noted between the study of geography and the study of history?
3. How sharp is the physical separation of Europe from Asia and Africa?
4. Explain the significance in European history of (a) the Mediterranean Sea, (b) the European mountain systems, (c) the European rivers.
5. Of what importance has climate been in history?
6. To what historical factors has agriculture been related over the centuries?

Key Discussion Sentences

Certain topographical features of Europe have remained unchanged in historic times.

The Mediterranean Sea is unique among the world's bodies of water.

Since the end of the Ice Age, Europe has been one of the most favored places on the globe for human habitation.

Some of the most important older cities of Europe are on rivers or other bodies of water.

Agriculture depends on natural conditions but also on many other developments.

Identifications

"Europe"	the Urals	temperate zone
Caspian Gate	"little Ice Age"	Rhone River valley

1

Map Exercises

1. As suggested in the text, trace on the physical map, pp. 4–5, an imaginary line from Amsterdam eastward for about 3,500 miles, passing north of the Caspian Sea to the borders of western China. What is the outstanding feature that one notes in traveling along this line? Of what historical significance has this feature been?
2. Can you locate on the physical map, pp. 4–5, or on the maps on the front and back end papers of the text the major seas, rivers, straits, mountains, and cities mentioned?

1. Ancient Times: Greece, Rome, and Christianity

Study Questions

1. What justification is there for a "history of the modern world" to concentrate on the history of Europe?
2. How do we conventionally date the following: (a) "modern" times, (b) the Middle Ages, (c) classical Greco-Roman civilization, (d) ancient times? Why is "modern" a purely relative term?
3. What important changes took place in Europe after about 2000 B.C.?
4. For what major contributions are the Greeks remembered? the Romans?
5. Why was the coming of Christianity so important in the development of European civilization?

Key Discussion Sentences

Most of what we call "modern" civilization originated in Europe.

Europeans were by no means the pioneers of human civilization.

The Greeks proved to be as gifted a people as mankind has ever produced.

The distinctive aptitude of the Romans lay in organization, administration, government, and law.

It is impossible to exaggerate the importance of the coming of Christianity. It brought a new sense of human life and human unity.

It was for their political ideas that the Christians were most often denounced and persecuted.

Identifications

Neolithic age	Aristotle	Roman law
Indo-European	Alexander the Great	St. Augustine
"classical virtues"	*Pax Romana*	

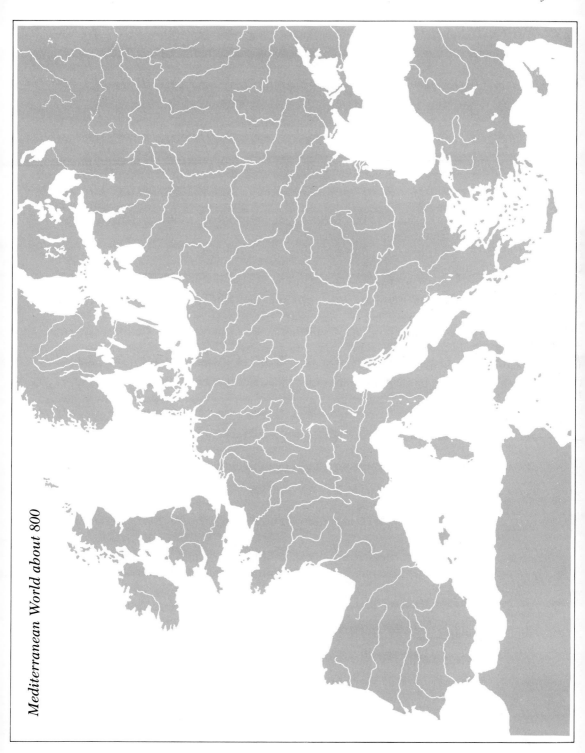

Mediterranean World about 800

Map Exercises

1. What were the approximate boundaries of the Roman Empire at its height? (See map, p. 21.)
2. Can you locate each of the places mentioned in Section 1?

2. *The Early Middle Ages: The Formation of Europe*

Study Questions

1. What factors contributed to the decline and breakup of the Roman Empire?
2. Describe and compare the three civilizations that confronted each other across the Mediterranean about A.D. 700.
3. Discuss the traditions and institutions of the Germanic tribes that invaded the Roman Empire.
4. Why could western Europe be said to be in the "Dark Ages" for a period of time after about A.D. 500? What role did the Christian church play at this time?
5. Describe the origins and accomplishments of Charlemagne's empire. What accounted for its fall?
6. In what sense was Europe assuming some of its modern political form by about A.D. 1000?

Key Discussion Sentences

It was in the half-millennium from the fifth to the tenth centuries that "Europe," as such emerged.

For internal and external reasons the Roman Empire in the West disintegrated in the fourth and fifth centuries A.D.

As a result of the barbarian invasions of the fifth century and the Arab conquests of the seventh century, the old unity of the Greco-Roman or Mediterranean world was broken.

Of the three civilizations that confronted each other across the Mediterranean about A.D. 700—the Byzantine Empire, the Arabic world, and Latin Christendom— Latin Christendom looked the least promising.

In the so-called Dark Ages, the Christian church was the one organized institution of political, spiritual, and cultural importance.

Under Charlemagne's empire, about A.D. 800, the West was once again temporarily united.

Identifications

Byzantine Empire	trial by battle	battle of Tours
Muhammad	Dark Ages	Charlemagne
Koran	"Petrine supremacy"	Great Schism of East
caliph	"Donation of Con-	and West
trial by ordeal	stantine"	

Map Exercises

1. On the outline map of Europe indicate the approximate boundaries about A.D. 800 of (a) Latin Christendom, (b) Greek Christendom, (c) the Muslim world. Suggested source: *A History of the Modern World*, p. 21.
2. Can you locate each of the places mentioned in Section 2?

3. The High Middle Ages: Secular Civilization

Study Questions

1. What sweeping changes in the eleventh century enabled Europe to pull itself out of the Dark Ages?
2. How would you define feudalism? What were its origins?
3. Distinguish between (a) feudalism and the manorial system, (b) the lord-vassal relationship and the lord-serf relationship.
4. Compare the status of the medieval serf to that of a slave in ancient civilizations. What accounted for the virtual disappearance of slavery from medieval Europe?
5. Explain the role of commerce and of the towns in the High Middle Ages. What effects did each have on the rural countryside?
6. Describe the growth in the High Middle Ages of (a) royal power, (b) royal councils, (c) parliaments.

Key Discussion Sentences

Important changes began to take place in Europe in the eleventh century in agriculture, commerce, and political life.

A notable feature of feudalism was its mutual or reciprocal character.

The manorial system was an agricultural base on which the ruling class was supported.

The new towns struggled to establish themselves as little self-governing republics.

The spirit of the medieval economy was to prevent competition.

The three centuries of the High Middle Ages laid foundations both for order and for freedom.

Identifications

High Middle Ages	three-field system	merchant guild
vassal	"law merchant"	craft guild
Hugh Capet	imperial free cities	Magna Carta
manor	Hanse	"estates of the realm"
serf		

4. The High Middle Ages: The Church

Study Questions

1. What fundamental institutional changes took place in the church in the eleventh century before Gregory VII? under Gregory VII? in the thirteenth century under Innocent III?
2. Discuss with reference to the intellectual life of the High Middle Ages (a) the origins and nature of the universities, (b) the contributions of Arab learning, (c) the role of the scholastic philosophers.
3. How does the painting by Sassetta (p. 41) reveal the medieval way of portraying the external world?
4. Describe the motives and results of (a) the European crusades to the Holy Land, (b) crusading activities elsewhere.
5. Describe the civilization of Europe by A.D. 1300. How might it be compared with that of the Arab world? the Chinese Empire of this period?

Key Discussion Sentences

In the High Middle Ages, religion permeated every aspect of life.

The church as a human institution was virtually "created" in the eleventh century.

The scholastics sought to reconcile the body of Greek and Arabic learning to the Christian faith.

New threats to Europe arose after 1250, but Europe was now capable of resistance.

By 1300 medieval Europe shared many common institutions, religious and secular.

In the very "disorder" of Europe there was also a kind of freedom, and a dynamism that promoted change.

Identifications

Holy Roman Empire	sacraments	Anselm
Cluniac reformers	"to go to Canossa"	Abelard
quarrel between Gregory VII and Henry IV	Innocent III	Aristotle
	Fourth Lateran Council	"scholastic" philosophers
	dogma	
excommunication	transubstantiation	Thomas Aquinas

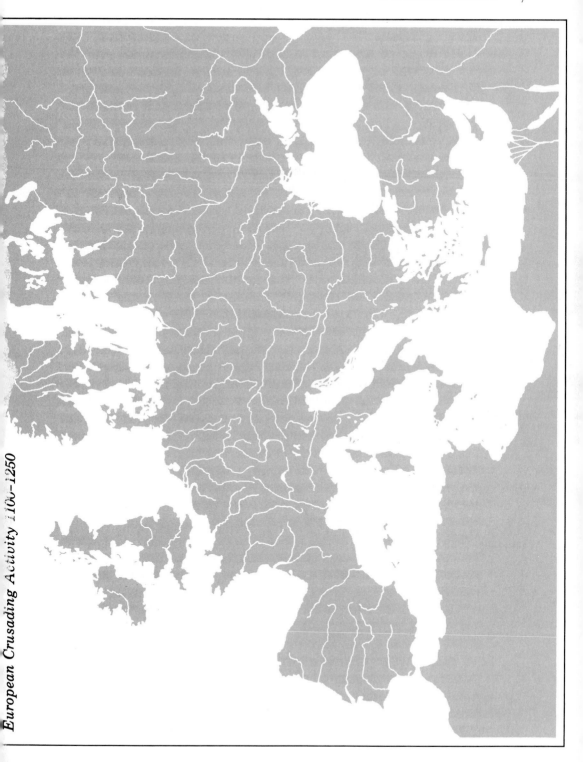

European Crusading Activity 1100–1250

Map Exercises

1. On the outline map on the preceding page, sketch an approximate picture of European crusading activity from about 1100 to 1250. Suggested source: *A History of the Modern World*, p. 44.
2. Can you locate each of the places mentioned in Section 4?

GENERAL ESSAY QUESTIONS FOR CHAPTER I

1. It is generally agreed that by 1300 the rise of a distinctively European civilization was an accomplished fact. What were the most important contributions made to that civilization by (a) Greece, (b) Rome, (c) the early Middle Ages, (d) the High Middle Ages?
2. How did Christianity affect the spiritual, intellectual, and institutional development of Europe (a) in the ancient world, (b) from the fifth to the tenth century, (c) from the eleventh to the end of the thirteenth century?
3. Compare economic, political, and social changes in Europe in the High Middle Ages with religious, intellectual, and cultural changes in the same period.

GENERAL DISCUSSION PASSAGES FOR CHAPTER I

Since our own age is one in which much depends on political decision, we think of this history as political history in the broadest sense, in that matters of many kinds, such as religion, economics, social welfare, and international relations, have presented themselves as public questions requiring public action by responsible citizens or governments. (Preface, p. xvi)

It is the business of geography not merely to describe and map the earth and its various areas, but to study the changing relationships between human activities and the surrounding environment. (p. 1)

It can be argued that Europe is not a continent at all, but a cultural conception arising from felt differences from Asia and Africa. (p. 2)

There is no geographical determinism. Climate and environment not only set limits but provide opportunities for what human beings can do. (p. 6)

In human terms, when one converts space into time, Europe has not been such a small place after all. (p. 7)

Over the centuries Europe developed an overwhelming impact on other continents and on other cultures in America, Asia, and Africa, sometimes destroying them, sometimes stimulating or enlivening them, and always presenting them with problems of resistance or adaptation. (p. 9)

Whatever their backgrounds, and willingly or not, all peoples in the modern world have been caught up in the process of modernization, or "development," which has usually meant acquiring some of the skills and powers first exhibited by Europeans. (p. 9)

Movements for social change may be slow and gradual, or revolutionary and catastrophic, but movement of some kind is universal. Everywhere today there is a drive for more equality in a variety of ways. (p. 10)

The Greeks were the first to write history as a subject distinct from myth and legend. (p. 12)

The idea that no ruler, no government, and no institution is too mighty to rise above moral criticism opened the way to a dynamic and progressive way of living in the West. (p. 17)

Some historical periods are so dynamic that a person who lives to be fifty years old can remember sweeping changes within his or her own lifetime. This is true of both the contemporary age and the period that began in Europe in the eleventh century. (p. 26)

If any historical generalization may be made safely, it may be safely said that any society that believes reason to threaten its foundations will suppress reason. (p. 42)

Many have asked why China did not generate, as medieval Europe did, the forces that ultimately led to the modern scientific and industrial world. (p. 44)

II.
THE UPHEAVAL IN CHRISTENDOM, 1300–1560
SECTIONS 5–10, pp. 46–93
PICTURE ESSAY, pp. 95–105

5. Disasters of the Fourteenth Century

Study Questions

1. How would you summarize the disasters that afflicted European society in the fourteenth century?
2. Describe the social and political consequences of the Black Death with special reference to (a) the peasants, (b) the upper classes, (c) royal governments, (d) European population trends.
3. What are the most striking features of the population trends shown in the chart on p. 48?
4. What difficulties and challenges did the church and papacy face in the fourteenth century? How were they resolved?
5. Discuss the aims, accomplishments, and outcome of the conciliar movement.

Key Discussion Sentences

Social and political unrest in the fourteenth century led to symptoms of mass neurosis.

At the close of the thirteenth century the church stood at its height. After 1300, the national monarchies were strong enough to assert themselves and to clash with the church.

The division in the papacy in the fourteenth century led to a sense of religious insecurity.

By 1450 the popes had triumphed over the challenge of the conciliar movement.

Identifications

Black Death	Hundred Years' War	Philip the Fair
''jacqueries''	Boniface VIII	John Wyclif
Wat Tyler's rebellion	*Unam Sanctam*	John Huss

"Babylonian Captivity"
  of the church
Great Schism of the
  West

"annates"
Council of Constance
Martin V

Pragmatic Sanction of
  Bourges

6. *The Renaissance in Italy*

PICTURE ESSAY: THE FLORENCE OF THE RENAISSANCE
(pp. 95–105)

Study Questions

1. Why is "Renaissance" in some ways an erroneous term? What relationship may be pointed out between the modern world and the Middle Ages? the modern world and the Renaissance?
2. Explain the new attitudes and "new conception of life itself" that arose in Renaissance Italy. How would you contrast Renaissance attitudes with those of the Middle Ages?
3. How were Italian Renaissance attitudes reflected in "humanism"? What attitude did the humanists take toward the Middle Ages? toward the Greeks and Romans? Why?
4. How was a fusion of "civic consciousness and humanism" demonstrated in the careers of Salutati and Bruni?
5. Discuss the impact of the Renaissance on education and on manners. How was the idea of the "courtier" and the "gentleman" developed in this age?
6. Discuss the special contributions made by Machiavelli to politics and political thought. What motivated his writings? How would you evaluate his conclusions? (See also p. 308.)
7. How do the painting by Bellini (p. 64) and the illustrations and discussion in the Picture Essay (pp. 95–105) convey a sense of the art and civic life of Renaissance Florence?

Key Discussion Sentences

The Renaissance marked a new era in thought and feelings by which Europe and its institutions were in the long run to be transformed.

It was in Renaissance Italy that an almost purely "secular" attitude first appeared.

What captivated the Italians of the Renaissance was a sense of the vast range of human powers.

The growing preoccupation with things human may be traced in Renaissance painting, architecture, and sculpture.

Florence produced an amazing number of leading figures of the Italian Renaissance.

If the humanists made a cult of antiquity, it was because they saw kindred spirits in it and sensed a relevancy for their own time.

The Renaissance had tangible and lasting effects on education.

The Renaissance failed to develop effective political institutions.

Machiavelli produced the first purely secular treatise on politics.

Identifications

Quattrocento	Leonardo da Vinci	Castiglione
Medici family	Raphael	*Last Supper*
virtú	Michelangelo	*Book of the Courtier*
condottiere	Lorenzo Valla	*The Prince*
Petrarch	Pico della Mirandola	

7. *The Renaissance outside Italy*

Study Questions

1. How did the Renaissance in Europe north of the Alps differ from the Renaissance in Italy?
2. What special religious aspects were there to the northern Renaissance? Of what significance were (a) the spread of mysticism, (b) the development of religious groups outside the clergy?
3. How did the scientific and mathematical interests of the northern Renaissance resemble Italian Renaissance ideas?
4. Explain the contributions of Erasmus to his age. How does Holbein's portrait of Erasmus (p. 64) reflect Erasmus as a scholar and as a person?

Key Discussion Sentences

Outside Italy people were much less conscious of any sudden break with the Middle Ages.

The religious interests of the northern Renaissance were reflected both in religious scholarship and in the religious impulse of individual mystics.

The interest in the human potential to understand and control physical nature developed mostly in the northern Renaissance.

Erasmus was the greatest of all the northern humanists and indeed the most notable figure of the entire humanist movement.

Identifications

Christian humanism	Meister Eckhart	*Imitation of Christ*
Regiomontanus	Thomas à Kempis	*Praise of Folly*

Nicholas of Cusa
Copernicus
Paracelsus
Dr. Faustus
Gerard Groote

Sisters of the Common
   Life
Brothers of the Com-
   mon Life

Handbook of a Chris-
   tian Knight
Modern Devotion

8. *The New Monarchies*

Study Questions

1. Describe the origins, nature, and accomplishments of the New Monarchies with reference to (a) England, (b) France, (c) Spain, (d) the Holy Roman Empire.
2. What role did the following play in the growth of royal authority: (a) the towns, (b) new weapons, (c) the revival of Roman law?
3. How did Charles V become the most powerful ruler of his day? What attitudes did Europeans take toward the Habsburg supremacy?
4. What political and nonpolitical developments may be cited as important to the emergence of Protestantism?

Key Discussion Sentences

After the middle of the fifteenth century, the New Monarchs resumed the interrupted labors of the medieval kings, strengthening royal authority over feudal authority and laying the basis for national territorial states.

In Spain, the New Monarchy took the form not so much of political centralization as of unification around the church.

In the Holy Roman Empire, Maximilian (1493–1519) tried unsuccessfully to introduce centralizing principles.

Charles V (1519–1556) was beyond all comparison the most powerful ruler of his day.

Identifications

Henry VII
Louis XI
Ferdinand and Isabella
Maximilian I
Charles V
Wars of the Roses

Tudors
"livery and mainte-
   nance"
Star Chamber
Concordat of Bologna

Spanish Inquisition
conquest of Granada
Moriscos
Marranos
imperial knights

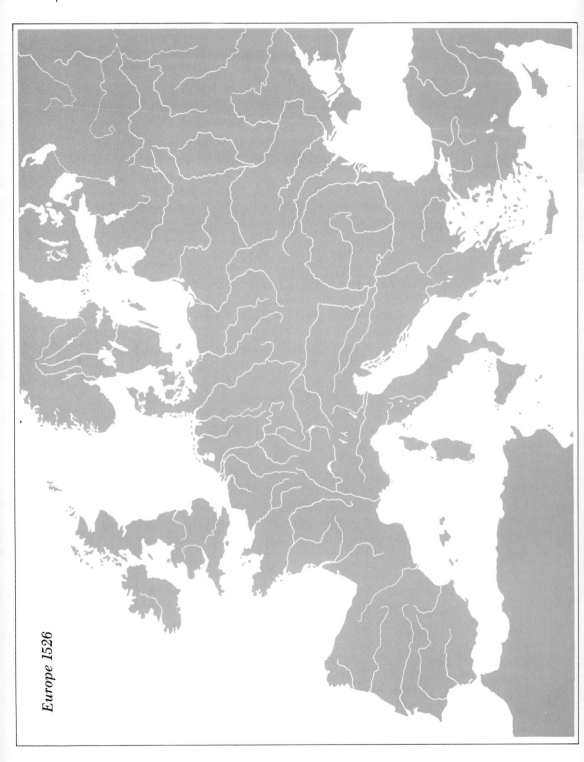

Europe 1526

Map Exercises

1. On the outline map of Europe, "Europe 1526," indicate (a) the territory ruled by the Habsburg family in 1526 and (b) the boundaries of the Holy Roman Empire at the time. What disposition did Charles V make of his territories in 1556? Suggested source: *A History of the Modern World*, pp. 72–73.
2. Can you locate each of the places mentioned in Section 8?

9. *The Protestant Reformation*

Study Questions

1. Describe the sources of dissatisfaction that contributed to the sixteenth-century religious upheaval.
2. What was revolutionary about Luther's position on religious authority? What political support did he find for his program?
3. How did Lutheranism become involved in political and social upheaval? How did Luther modify his position in the face of these events?
4. How did Calvin differ from Luther in training, background, and personality? How did Calvinism resemble and differ from Lutheranism?
5. Explain the special course of the Reformation in England. What changes occurred under Henry VIII? Edward VI? Mary? Elizabeth?
6. What common doctrines and beliefs were shared by all Protestants? What observations may be made about the results of the Protestant Reformation in Europe by 1560?
7. Discuss the thesis that one of the chief motivations for the Protestant Reformation was economic.

Key Discussion Sentences

Three streams of discontent contributed to the religious upheaval of the sixteenth century.

The leaders of the Reformation were religious revolutionaries, not partisans of "freedom of religion" or of "religious toleration."

Horrified at the way in which religious revolution passed into social revolution, Luther defined his own position more conservatively.

Calvin and Luther differed on (a) the idea of "predestination" and (b) the relationship between church and state.

In England the government broke with the Roman Catholic church before adopting any Protestant principles.

By 1560, although religious issues were far from settled, the chief Protestant doctrines had been affirmed; and geographically, Protestantism had made many conquests.

By 1600 socio-religious radicalism was reduced to an undercurrent.

In the Protestant Reformation, economic conditions seemed less decisive than religious convictions and political circumstances.

Identifications

Protestant
"justification by faith"
indulgences
Ninety-Five Theses
transubstantiation
Peasants' Revolt
Anabaptists

Schmalkaldic War
Peace of Augsburg
cuius regio eius religio
Ecclesiastical Reser-
    vation
*Institutes of the Chris-
    tian Religion*

Michael Servetus
"predestination"
Henry VIII
Act of Supremacy
Anglican church
Thirty-Nine Articles

10. Catholicism Reformed and Reorganized

Study Questions

1. Why are the terms "Catholic Reformation" and "Counter Reformation" both justified?
2. Explain the purpose, nature, and accomplishments of the Council of Trent. How did it reaffirm Catholic doctrine? How did it attempt to reform church abuses?
3. Describe the changes in Catholicism with reference to (a) new religious attitudes, (b) missionary activities, (c) the role of the Jesuits, (d) the "reforming popes."
4. How was the fate of European religion eventually to be worked out?

Key Discussion Sentences

The reform decrees of the Council of Trent might have remained ineffectual had not a renewed sense of religious seriousness grown up within Catholicism at the same time.

It was in Spain that much of the new Catholic feeling and missionary spirit first developed.

By 1560 the Catholic church had devised practical machinery for a counteroffensive against Protestantism.

Identifications

"episcopal" movement
justification by works
    and faith

Paul III
St. Vincent de Paul
St. Ignatius Loyola

"ultramontanism"
Index of Prohibited
    Books

| Vulgate | Society of Jesus | Spanish Inquisition |
| pluralism | *Spiritual Exercises* | Roman Inquisition |

Map Exercise

1. On the outline map of Europe, "State Religions in Europe about 1560," indicate the state religions in Europe at this time, using different shading for Lutheranism, Anglicanism, Calvinism, and Roman Catholicism. In which areas was Calvinism the dominant religion? Where was it a minority religion? Suggested source: *A History of the Modern World*, pp. 86–87.

GENERAL ESSAY QUESTIONS FOR CHAPTER II

1. In the age of religious revolution and secularization from 1300 to 1560, Europe began to take on its modern outlines. What major developments accounted for this historic change?
2. Explain whether it is correct to say that a "religious revolution" had taken place in Europe by 1560.
3. What common elements and what distinctive differences do you see in comparing the following: (a) the Italian Renaissance, (b) the Renaissance outside Italy, (c) the Protestant Reformation, and (d) the Catholic Counter Reformation?
4. In what ways did (a) the Middle Ages, (b) the Renaissance, and (c) the Reformation help create the "modern world"?

GENERAL DISCUSSION PASSAGES FOR CHAPTER II

If in our time there has come to be such a thing as a world civilization, it is because all the world's great traditional cultures have been increasingly secularized. They have not rejected their ancestral religions, but they have developed a variety of activities outside the sphere of religion. (p. 46)

The effects of the Italian Renaissance, though much modified with the passage of time, were evident in the books and art galleries of Europe and America, and in the architecture of their cities, until the revolution of "modern" art in the early twentieth century. (p. 53)

With the Renaissance, literature became a kind of calling and also a consideration of moral philosophy in the widest sense, raising questions of how human beings should adjust to the world, what a good life could be or ought to be, and where the genuine and ultimate rewards of living were to be found. (p. 58)

With many of the Renaissance humanists, history took on a utility that it had had for the Greeks and Romans and was to retain in the future in Europe and eventually in America: the function of heightening a sentiment not yet of nationalism but of collective civic consciousness or group identity. It was meant to arouse its readers to a life of commitment and participation. (p. 59)

What really happens, said Machiavelli, is that effective rulers and governments act only in their own political interest. They keep faith or break it, observe treaties or repudiate them, are merciful or ruthless, forthright or sly, peaceable or aggressive, according to their estimates of their own political needs. He had diagnosed the new era with considerable insight. (p. 61)

Faust was rumored to have sold his soul to the devil in return for knowledge and power. In the legend of Faust, later generations were to see a symbol of the inordinate striving of modern man. When Oswald Spengler published his *Decline of the West* in 1918, he called the European civilization whose doom he prophesied "Faustian." (pp. 63–64)

Among Erasmus' virtues was a critical and reforming zeal which, hating nobody, worked through trying to make people think. (p. 67)

Calvinism was far from democratic in any modern sense, being rather of an almost aristocratic outlook, in that those who sensed themselves to be God's chosen few felt free to dictate to the common run of mankind. Yet in many ways Calvinism entered into the development of what became democracy. (p. 82)

It is possible that Protestantism, by casting a glow of religious righteousness over a person's daily business and material prosperity, later contributed to the economic success of Protestant peoples, but it does not seem that economic forces were of any distinctive importance in the first stages of Protestantism. (pp. 86–87)

The Council of Trent (1545–1563) shaped the destiny of modern Catholicism. It was not until the Second Vatican Council in the 1960s that some of the main decisions made at Trent were substantially modified. (p. 88)

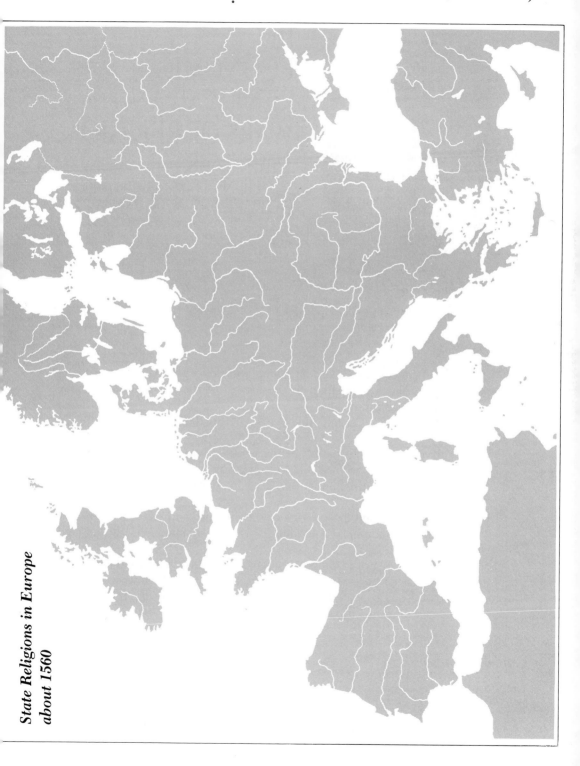

*State Religions in Europe
about 1560*

III.
ECONOMIC RENEWAL AND WARS OF RELIGION, 1560–1648
SECTIONS 11–16, pp. 106–149
PICTURE ESSAY, pp. 151–159

11. *The Opening of the Atlantic*

PICTURE ESSAY: THE WORLD OVERSEAS (pp. 151–159)

Study Questions

1. Of what significance was Vasco da Gama's discovery of a sea route to the East? Why was there opposition to the arrival of the Portuguese in India? How did the Portuguese meet it?
2. How did Columbus react to his "discovery"? How did others in Spain regard the new land?
3. How would you assess the nature of the Spanish empire in America? What negative and positive aspects would you mention?
4. Compare and contrast the empires created by Portugal in the East and by Spain in America.
5. How did the voyages and discoveries of the fifteenth and sixteenth centuries add to existing geographical knowledge? (See also maps, p. 108 and pp. 302–303.)
6. From the paintings on pp. 111 and 113 and from the illustrations and discussion in the Picture Essay (pp. 151–159) what conclusions may be drawn about the significance of the European discoveries for Europe, and for the relationships of Europeans with non-European peoples?

Key Discussion Sentences

The Portuguese created in the East the first of Europe's commercial-colonial empires.

Christopher Columbus's voyage led to the somewhat disappointing discovery of America.

In the populous and civilized East, Europeans were never more than transients; in America, Europeans established their own civilization.

The opening of the Atlantic reoriented Europe.

Europe itself was transformed by its overseas ventures.

The consequences of the discoveries were favorable for the Europeans but devastating for the native peoples involved.

Identifications

da Gama	treaty of 1494	encomienda
Albuquerque	*conquistadores*	mestizos
St. Francis Xavier	Black Legend	Potosí
Magellan	viceroyalty	University of Lima

Map Exercises

1. Study the map on p. 108. Can you trace the principal voyages and explorations to the East and to America described in the text? How did the Spanish and the Portuguese "divide" the globe in 1494?
2. By studying the maps on pp. 302–303, compare the extent of European geographical knowledge in 1492, in 1523, and in the eighteenth century.
3. Can you locate each of the places mentioned in Section 11?

12. The Commercial Revolution

Study Questions

1. What important economic changes in the early modern centuries does the term "Commercial Revolution" signify?
2. Describe the growth of European population in the sixteenth century and the nature of this growth. How can Appendix III of the text be used to supplement your answer?
3. Explain the origins, nature, and effects of the "putting out" or "domestic" system. Of what importance were the needs of the military in the rise of capitalism? What change in attitudes could be noted toward the lending of money at interest?
4. Explain the general nature and purpose of mercantilism, citing examples of mercantilist policies and regulations. What comparison may be made between mercantilism and the New Monarchies?

Key Discussion Sentences

In the economic adjustments taking place, the change in trade routes, the growth in population, and the rise in prices were each important.

The Commercial Revolution signified in general the rise of a capitalist economy and the transition from a town-centered to a nation-centered economic system.

In the age of commercial capitalism, the key person in business was the merchant, not the producer.

Mercantilist practices and policies were designed to build a strong and self-sufficient national economy.

Identifications

"price revolution"   "usury"   Statute of Artificers
guild   commercial capitalism   internal tariffs
entrepreneur   mercantilism   chartered trading
Medici   favorable balance of   companies
Fugger   trade

13. Changing Social Structures

Study Questions

1. Describe the economic classes emerging in Europe in the early modern centuries. How did the economic changes of the sixteenth century affect each class?
2. What accounted for the new demand for education?
3. Why did the economic changes of these years affect the rural classes of eastern Europe and of western Europe differently? With what consequences?

Key Discussion Sentences

The classes of Europe, broadly defined, took on forms in the early modern centuries that were to last until the industrial era of the nineteenth and twentieth centuries.

The poor, if not positively worse off than in former times, gained the least from the great economic developments under way.

Education in the latter part of the sixteenth century took on an altogether new importance for the social system.

Social classes were influenced by economic forces, education, and the action of governments.

It was in the sixteenth century that a great difference developed between eastern and western Europe.

Identifications

"social structure"	*robot*	"plebeians"
yeoman	hidalgo	"hereditary subjection"
Poor Law of 1601	*collège*	Junker
bourgeois	Ursuline sisters	

14. The Crusade of Catholic Spain: The Dutch and English

Study Questions

1. Why could Philip II rightly regard himself as an international figure? Why was Spain ideally suited to be the instrument of Philip's ambitions?
2. How would you describe and characterize the general state of political and religious affairs in Europe in the first years of Philip's reign? What conflict existed between religious and national loyalties?
3. How permanent were the triumphs of Philip and of the Catholic cause in the years 1567 to 1572?
4. Explain the political, economic, and religious issues that entered into the revolt of the Netherlands. How did the revolt merge with the international political and religious struggles in Europe?
5. How would you analyze the reasons for Spain's decline?

Key Discussion Sentences

Philip II took upon himself the leadership of a vast Catholic counteroffensive.

The Netherlands' revolt against Philip II was political and religious at the same time; as the years went by it became more and more an economic struggle.

The Netherlands' revolt, which began as a struggle against Spain, became part of the international conflict of the age.

Although Spain was to remain the most formidable military power of Europe for another half-century, by 1600 its internal decline had already begun.

Spain suffered from the very circumstances that made it great. The crusading qualities most useful in leading the Counter Reformation were not those on which a modern society could easily be built.

Identifications

Austrian and Spanish Habsburgs	Council of Troubles	Prince of Parma
siglo de oro	Duke of Norfolk	Union of Utrecht
Escorial	Lepanto	Sir Francis Drake
	William the Silent	*armada católica*

Joyeuse Entrée   Mary Queen of Scots   Twelve Years' Truce
Duke of Alva   Don Juan

Map Exercises

1. On the outline map of Europe, "Europe 1526," used earlier for Section 8, show the division of Charles V's empire in 1556 between the Spanish and Austrian Habsburgs. What other territories did Philip II rule outside Europe? in Europe after 1580? Suggested source: *A History of the Modern World*, pp. 72–73.
2. Study the map in the text on p. 130. How were the Low Countries divided as a result of events in the sixteenth and seventeenth centuries?
3. Can you locate each of the places mentioned in Section 14?

15. *The Disintegration and Reconstruction of France*

Study Questions

1. To what extent did the monarchy succeed in imposing unity on France by the second half of the sixteenth century? What is meant by the term "feudal" as used after the Middle Ages?
2. Describe the background, nature, and outcome of the civil and religious wars in France in the sixteenth century.
3. Of what long-range significance was the position taken by the *politiques* in the civil wars in France?
4. How did Henry IV come to the throne in 1589? What is the deeper meaning of the remark, "Paris is well worth a Mass"?
5. How did Henry IV attempt to settle the religious issue? Of what significance was his reign for the development of the French monarchy?
6. How would you assess the objectives and accomplishments of Cardinal Richelieu?

Key Discussion Sentences

To the existing disunity in France in the sixteenth century, religious differences were added.

The wars of religion in France, from 1562 to 1598, were not only religious but political.

The *politiques* maintained that no religious doctrine was important enough to justify everlasting war.

From the disorders of the religious wars in France germinated the ideas of royal absolutism and the sovereign state.

Under Henry IV (1589–1610), the foundations of Bourbon absolutism were laid.

Cardinal Richelieu worked to further the interests of the state, not those of the church.

Identifications

"boy kings"	*politiques*	parlement
Huguenot	St. Bartholomew's Day	Estates-General
Catherine de' Medici	Massacre	rebellion of La Ro-
Admiral de Coligny	Jean Bodin	chelle
"three Henrys"	Edict of Nantes	Peace of Alais

16. The Thirty Years' War, 1618–1648: The Disintegration of Germany

Study Questions

1. How had the Peace of Augsburg attempted to settle the religious question in the German states? What developments upset those arrangements?
2. How may one attempt to analyze the issues of the Thirty Years' War? How did European rivalries and ambitions become linked to the conflict within Germany?
3. Sketch briefly the events associated with each of the major phases of the Thirty Years' War.
4. Summarize and evaluate the Peace of Westphalia with respect to (a) the religious settlement, (b) territorial changes, (c) constitutional issues within the Holy Roman Empire. Of what significance was the Peace of Westphalia for modern international relations?
5. How would you evaluate the broad significance of the Thirty Years' War and the Peace of Westphalia? What seems to have been the net result of the wars of religion?

Key Discussion Sentences

The Thirty Years' War was in part a German religious war and in part a German civil war fought over constitutional issues in the Holy Roman Empire.

As an international war, it was a conflict principally between (1) France and the Habsburgs and (2) Spain and the Dutch.

The Peace of Westphalia represented a general checkmate to the Catholic cause in Germany.

The Holy Roman Empire as an effective political entity was demolished by the Peace of Westphalia.

The Peace of Westphalia marked the advent in international law of the modern system of independent sovereign states.

With the close of the Thirty Years' War, the wars of religion came to an end; religion was never again an important issue in the political affairs of Europe as a whole.

Identifications

Holy Roman Empire	Frederick V	Edict of Restitution
Peace of Augsburg	Protestant Union	Wallenstein
Ecclesiastical Reser-	"defenestration of	Gustavus Adolphus
vation	Prague"	Oxenstierna
Matthias	battle of the White	Peace of Westphalia
Ferdinand II	Mountain	"German liberties"

Map Exercises

1. On the outline map of Europe draw the approximate boundaries of the major European states in 1648 after the Peace of Westphalia. Suggested source: *A History of the Modern World*, pp. 146–147.
2. Can you locate each of the places mentioned in Section 16?

GENERAL ESSAY QUESTIONS FOR CHAPTER III

1. How did the years 1560–1648 bring to a close the religious revolution inaugurated earlier? Discuss with special reference to developments in Spain, the Netherlands, England, France, the Holy Roman Empire, and Europe as a whole.
2. Explain how in the age of religious upheaval, from the beginnings of the Protestant Reformation to 1648, religious issues blended with political, constitutional, economic, and social questions.
3. Describe the evolution of early modern capitalism, explaining (a) its origins in the Middle Ages, (b) the impact of the overseas discoveries in the sixteenth century, (c) the relationship of emergent capitalism to the various social classes.

GENERAL DISCUSSION PASSAGES FOR CHAPTER III

Often, in the wars of religion from about 1560 to 1648, the ideological lines became blurred, as Catholics lent aid to Protestants, or vice versa, somewhat as ideological issues in our own day tend to be confused. (p. 106)

"Discovery" means the bringing of newly found countries within the habitual knowledge of the society from which the discoverer comes. It was the Europeans who thus "discovered" the rest of the world between about 1450 and 1600. (p. 108)

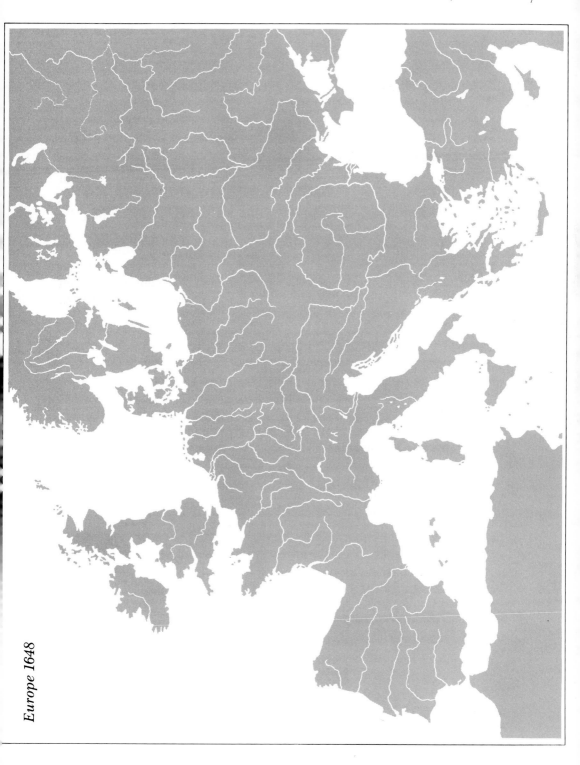

Europe 1648

By 1992, as Native American and African American voices were increasingly heard, the fifth centennial of Columbus's first voyage was seen as little to celebrate. (p. 107)

The "price revolution" of the sixteenth century was so slow as to be hardly comparable to the kinds of inflation known in the twentieth century. (p. 115)

The diplomats who assembled at Westphalia represented independent powers that recognized no superior or common tie. No longer did anyone pretend that Europe had any significant unity, religious or political. (p. 148)

The effects of fire, disease, undernourishment, homelessness, and exposure in the seventeenth century were the more terrible because of the lack of means to combat them. The horrors of modern war are not wholly different from horrors that men and women have experienced in the past. (p. 149)

With the overseas discoveries, Europeans took increasing pride in their understanding of the world. There was much speculation on the diversity of human races and cultures, which sometimes led to a new kind of race consciousness on the part of Europeans, and sometimes to a cultural relativism in which European ways were seen as only one variant of human behavior as a whole. (p. 151)

IV.
THE
ESTABLISHMENT OF
WEST-EUROPEAN
LEADERSHIP
SECTIONS 17–22, pp. 160–197
PICTURE ESSAY, pp. 199–208

17. *The Grand Monarque and the Balance of Power*

Study Questions

1. What observations may be made about the significance of western Europe in the development of modern civilization since about 1650?
2. What general statements may be made about the nature of Louis XIV's rule in France and about the role of France in European affairs during his reign?
3. Why did Louis XIV's foreign policy arouse the opposition of the rest of Europe?
4. Explain the nature of the "balance of power" that was employed against Louis XIV. Of what broad significance has the "balance of power" concept been in diplomatic history?

Key Discussion Sentences

The half-century following the Peace of Westphalia is often called the Age of Louis XIV.

No one else in modern history has held so powerful a position for so long a time as did Louis XIV.

Internationally, the consuming political question of the last decades of the seventeenth century in western Europe was the fate of the vast possessions of the Spanish crown.

The diplomatic technique used against "universal monarchy" and called into play against Louis XIV was the "balance of power."

Identifications

Grand Monarque	Charles II of Spain	"universal monarchy"
Sun King	Franche Comté	

18. *The Dutch Republic*

Study Questions

1. Describe Dutch cultural and commercial accomplishments in the seventeenth century.
2. How do the two paintings by Rembrandt (pp. 113 and 165) and the paintings by Vermeer and Moreelse (pp. 111 and 292) illustrate Dutch artistic achievements and Dutch intellectual, commercial, and colonial enterprises?
3. Explain the nature of government and of political life in the seventeenth-century Dutch Republic.
4. How did the Dutch and English come into conflict in the seventeenth century? With what results?
5. How did the Dutch become involved in conflict with Louis XIV? With what results?

Key Discussion Sentences

The Dutch were the most bourgeois of all peoples.

The seventeenth century was an age of great Dutch cultural achievements—in political writing, philosophy, science, and painting.

Throughout the century the Dutch engaged in vast commercial, colonial, and banking undertakings.

Politics in the Dutch Republic was a seesaw between the burghers and the princes of Orange, to whom the country owed most of its military security.

To offset the aggressive, expansionist policies of Louis XIV, the Dutch set into motion the mechanism of the balance of power.

Identifications

Estates-General of the United Provinces	William III	hereditary stadhold-erate
Arminians	English Navigation Act of 1651	Hugo Grotius
Bank of Amsterdam	English-Dutch wars	Baruch Spinoza
House of Orange	Treaty of Nimwegen	Christian Huyghens

19. *Britain: The Puritan Revolution*

Study Questions

1. What comparisons may be made between events in England in the seventeenth century and developments on the Continent?

2. Why did Parliament come into conflict with James I? with Charles I? How did the special nature of Parliament make its resistance effective?
3. How did the civil war begin? How did Cromwell emerge as ruler of England?
4. Describe the government of England under the Commonwealth and the Protectorate. What is meant by the regime of the "major generals"?
5. What policies did Cromwell follow toward Scotland? toward Ireland? in foreign affairs? toward the more radical elements emerging in England?
6. How would you evaluate Cromwell's role in English history?

Key Discussion Sentences

Neither to James I nor to his son Charles I would Parliament grant adequate revenue because it distrusted both.

Many members of Parliament were Puritans, dissatisfied with the Church of England.

Parliament had no sooner defeated the king than it fell out with its own army.

Though Cromwell professed a belief in parliamentary and constitutional government, he ruled as a dictator in behalf of a stern Puritan minority.

The Puritan Revolution failed to satisfy the most ardent and could not win over the truly conservative.

Identifications

Puritan	Archbishop Laud	Pride's Purge
Presbyterian	prerogative courts	the Rump
Anglican	ship money case	Levellers
James VI of Scotland	Long Parliament	Diggers
The True Law of Free Monarchy	Solemn League and Covenant	Fifth Monarchy Men
"tunnage and poundage"	Roundheads	Instrument of Government
	Independents	

20. Britain: The Triumph of Parliament

Study Questions

1. Explain the general nature of the Restoration in England. Of what significance was the legislation enacted by the Restoration Parliament?
2. How did religious matters again bring Parliament and king into conflict? What policies of James II precipitated the Revolution of 1688?
3. Summarize the legislation introduced after the Revolution of 1688. Of what significance was William's acceptance of the Bill of Rights?
4. Of what constitutional significance for England was the Revolution of 1688?

Why have writers in more recent times "deglorified" the revolution? Give arguments for and against this point of view.
5. What were the consequences of these events for Scotland? for Ireland?

Key Discussion Sentences

In 1660 not only the monarchy but also the Church of England and the Parliament were restored.

During the Restoration, Parliament enacted some far-reaching legislation on land tenure and taxation.

Not long after the Restoration, Parliament and king were again at odds. The issue was again religion.

In England the "Glorious Revolution" of 1688 might be said to have vindicated the principles of parliamentary government, the rule of law, and even the right of rebellion against tyranny.

The Irish emerged from the seventeenth century as the most repressed people of western Europe.

Identifications

Charles II
Dissenters
treaty of Dover
"declaration of indul-
    gence"
Test Act
Whigs and Tories

"trial of the seven
    bishops"
"Glorious Revolution"
William and Mary
battle of the Boyne
Bill of Rights

United Kingdom of
    Great Britain
Act of Settlement of
    1701
Toleration Act
"penal code" for
    Ireland

21. The France of Louis XIV, 1643–1715: The Triumph of Absolutism

PICTURE ESSAY: THE AGE OF GRANDEUR (pp. 199–208)

Study Questions

1. What factors accounted for France's leadership during the age of Louis XIV? Describe French cultural contributions and achievements in this age.
2. How did Louis XIV develop the "state" in its modern form? What is suggested as the deeper meaning of his reputed boast, "L'état, c'est moi"?
3. What arguments were used to justify the divine right of kings in the seventeenth century?
4. Discuss Louis XIV's (a) military and administrative reforms, (b) economic and financial policies, (c) religious policy.

The Atlantic World 1713

5. How would you assess the reign of Louis XIV from a purely domestic point of view?
6. From the illustrations and discussion in the Picture Essay (pp. 199–208), what does one learn about the meaning of the ''baroque'' style in architecture in this age? about French cultural influence in Europe in the seventeenth and eighteenth centuries?

Key Discussion Sentences

After the disorders of the religious wars in the sixteenth century, and after the Fronde in the seventeenth, many people welcomed a strong monarchy.

Louis XIV claimed to possess in his own person, as sovereign ruler, a monopoly over the lawmaking processes and the armed forces of the kingdom.

Louis XIV's absolutism rested on the theory of the divine right of kings, on Roman law, and on purely practical considerations.

Possibly the most fundamental reform undertaken by Louis XIV was to make war an activity of state.

Versailles completed the political and moral ruin of the French aristocracy as a class.

Finance was always the weak spot in the French monarchy.

Colbert worked to make France economically powerful and self-sufficient.

Louis XIV considered religious unity necessary to the strength and dignity of his rule.

Identifications

parlements	intendants	Commercial Code
Fronde	councils of state	French East India
Cardinal Mazarin	tax farmers	Company
Bishop Bossuet	Colbert	revocation of the Edict
divine right of kings	Five Great Farms	of Nantes
Versailles		

22. The Wars of Louis XIV: The Peace of Utrecht, 1713

Study Questions

1. Describe Louis XIV's foreign policy in the years prior to the War of the Spanish Succession. What form did his activities take in Alsace and Lorraine?
2. What features of the War of the Spanish Succession made it distinctive? Why was the war fought?

3. Summarize the main developments of the war. What motives prompted each state to continue to fight?
4. What were the major provisions of the Treaty of Utrecht? On what basis were differences between the great powers settled?

Key Discussion Sentences

From the outset of his reign, Louis XIV pursued a vigorous foreign policy.

The War of the Spanish Succession was the first major modern war that could be called a "world war" and was unique in other respects as well.

Never had the political balance within Europe been so threatened as when Louis XIV sought to accept the Spanish throne and territories for his grandson.

The old objective of William III, to prevent domination of Europe by France, was realized at last.

The Treaty of Utrecht left France and Great Britain as the two most vigorous powers of Europe.

Identifications

War of Devolution
"Dutch War"
Treaty of Nimwegen
chambres de réunion
War of the League of
    Augsburg
Peace of Ryswick

Charles II of Spain
"The Pyrenees exist no
    longer"
William III
John Churchill, Duke
    of Marlborough
Philip V of Spain

Grand Alliance of 1701
Prince Eugene of
    Savoy
treaties of Utrecht and
    Rastadt
asiento
"Dutch barrier"

Map Exercises

1. On the outline map of Europe and the Americas ("The Atlantic World") show the major territorial changes made by the Treaty of Utrecht. Identify (a) the territories belonging to the Spanish crown in 1701, (b) the territories that stayed with Spain under the Bourbon Philip V, (c) the territories that went to the Austrian Habsburgs, (d) the territories that went to Britain from Spain and from France. Suggested source: *A History of the Modern World*, pp. 196 and 328.
2. Can you locate each of the places mentioned in Section 22?

GENERAL ESSAY QUESTIONS FOR CHAPTER IV

1. France and England took different political and constitutional paths in the course of the seventeenth century. Compare and contrast internal developments in the two countries during this period.
2. Why is it reasonable to speak of the second half of the seventeenth century

as the Age of Louis XIV? What may be said of the Dutch and the English in this same period?

3. How was the balance-of-power concept used to check (a) the Habsburg bid for supremacy in the Thirty Years' War and (b) Louis XIV's bid for "universal monarchy" in the late seventeenth and early eighteenth centuries?

GENERAL DISCUSSION PASSAGES FOR CHAPTER IV

If the reader were to take a map of Europe, set a compass on the city of Paris, and draw a circle with a radius of five hundred miles, a zone would be marked out from which much of modern or "Western" civilization has radiated since about 1650. (p. 160)

The term "balance of power," which came into general use in the seventeenth century, has been employed ever since in different though related senses. (p. 162)

English classical literature, rugged in form but deep in content, vigorous yet subtle in insight, majestic, abundant, and sonorous in expression, was almost the reverse of French classical writing, with its virtues of order, economy, propriety, and graceful precision. (p. 170)

Government in England remained strong but came under parliamentary control. This determined the character of modern England and launched into the history of Europe and of the world the great movement of liberalism and representative institutions. (p. 171)

The Puritan Revolution, like others, produced its extremists. (p. 175)

Democratic ideas after the Puritan Revolution were generally rejected as "levelling." They were generally abandoned in England after 1660 or were cherished by obscure individuals. Such ideas, indeed, had a more continuous history in the English colonies in America. (p. 176)

The individual state, while representing law and order within its borders, has generally stood in a lawless and disorderly relation to other states since no higher monopoly of law and force has existed. The modern state, indeed, was created by the needs of peace at home and war abroad. (p. 185)

V.
THE TRANSFORMATION OF EASTERN EUROPE, 1648–1740
SECTIONS 23–27, pp. 210–250

23. *Three Aging Empires*

Study Questions

1. What major differences may be noted between eastern and western Europe in the seventeenth and eighteenth centuries?
2. Why may the Holy Roman Empire, the Republic of Poland, and the Ottoman Empire in the mid-seventeenth century be characterized as "old-fashioned" political organizations?
3. Describe the changes in the Holy Roman Empire brought about by (a) the Reformation, (b) the Thirty Years' War, (c) the Peace of Westphalia. What may be said about the ambitions and activities of various individual rulers in the empire?
4. What was distinctive about the political life of the Republic of Poland in the seventeenth century?
5. How would you characterize the nature of Ottoman rule in eastern Europe? What changes were taking place in the seventeenth century?

Key Discussion Sentences

In the seventeenth and eighteenth centuries the three "new" states of Austria, Prussia, and Russia were pushing aside the three older, large, and loosely built organizations—the Holy Roman Empire, the Republic of Poland, and the empire of the Ottoman Turks.

The Holy Roman Empire was described by Voltaire as neither holy, Roman, nor an empire.

Of the many ambitious German states after 1648, two states built by the skill and persistence of their rulers came forward after 1700—Austria and Prussia.

In Poland the monopoly of law and force, characteristic of the modern sovereign state, failed to develop.

To the Christian world the empire of the Ottoman Turks was a mystery as well as a terror.

The Ottoman Empire was a relatively tolerant empire, far more so than the states of Europe.

Identifications

"knights of the Empire"

Electors of the Holy Roman Empire

ius eundi in partes

"perpetual diet" of Regensburg

Hohenzollerns

Habsburgs

szlachta

liberum veto

"exploding" the diet

janissaries

"capitulations"

Map Exercises

1. On the outline maps of Europe indicate (a) in the upper panel the approximate boundaries about 1660 of the Holy Roman Empire, the Republic of Poland, and the Ottoman Empire; (b) in the lower panel the boundaries of the three "new" states—Austria, Prussia, and Russia—as they had developed by 1795; (c) in both panels the "Elbe-Trieste line" as described in the text. Suggested source: *A History of the Modern World*, pp. 216 and 222.
2. Can you locate each of the places mentioned in Section 23?

24. The Formation of an Austrian Monarchy

Study Questions

1. What were the major episodes and outcome of the conflict between the Habsburgs and the Turks from 1526 to 1739?
2. Describe the territorial boundaries of the Habsburg empire about 1740. In what sense was the empire "international"?
3. How successful were the Habsburgs in their efforts at consolidation and centralization? What steps did Charles VI take to guarantee the integrity of his territories?

Key Discussion Sentences

The House of Austria, in two or three generations after its humiliation at the Peace of Westphalia in 1648, acquired a new empire of very considerable proportions.

Though German influence was strong, the Habsburg empire was international or nonnational.

The Austrian monarchy remained a collection of territories held together by a personal union.

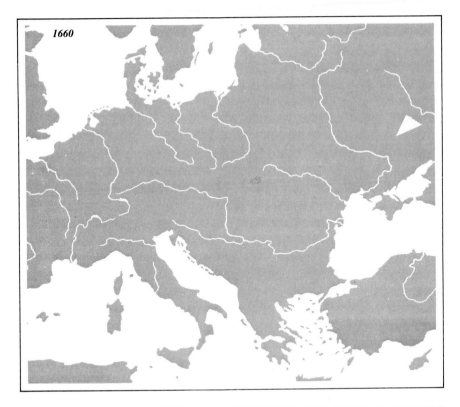

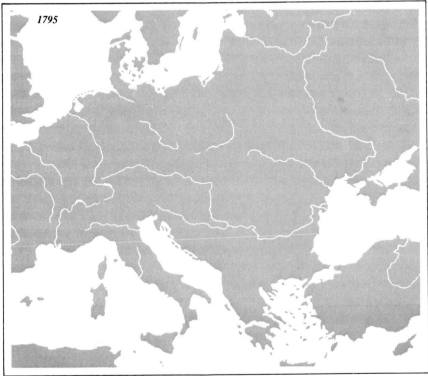

Aging Empires and New States

Identifications

Habsburg "hereditary provinces"	battle of Zenta	Prince Francis Rakoczy
siege of Vienna of 1683	Peace of Karlowitz	Magyars
Prince Eugene of Savoy	Treaty of Rastadt	Charles VI
	Peace of Belgrade	Pragmatic Sanction
	ius reformandi	

Map Exercises

1. Study the map on p. 222, "The Growth of the Austrian Monarchy 1521–1772," and the accompanying caption. What might be considered the nucleus of the empire? What were the boundaries of the empire in 1526? What was added in 1699? in 1713? by the first partition of Poland in 1772?
2. Can you locate each of the places mentioned in Section 24?

25. The Formation of Prussia

Study Questions

1. Explain the role of each of the Hohenzollern rulers from 1640 to 1740 in the formation of Prussia.
2. Describe the special characteristics of Prussia as it was developing in the seventeenth and eighteenth centuries. What observations may be made about (a) the army, (b) government and economic life, (c) the social development and economic structure of the country? What possible effects might Lutheranism have had on Prussian life?
3. Why did Frederick II's act of aggression seem to be an exception to the policies of his predecessors? What did he accomplish by this act?

Key Discussion Sentences

To connect and unify its disconnected territories became the underlying long-range policy of the Brandenburg house.

Until late in its history, Prussia was militaristic but not belligerent.

The economic life of Prussia grew up under government sponsorship, rather than by the enterprise of a venturesome business class.

The army had a profound effect on the social development and class structure of Prussia.

Judged simply as a human accomplishment, Prussia was a remarkable creation, a state made on a shoestring, a triumph of work and duty.

Identifications

Charles XII
"mark" or "march" of
  Brandenburg
Drang nach Osten
Hohenzollerns
Frederick William (the
  Great Elector)

Brandenburg-Prussia
king *in* Prussia
Frederick I
crown domain
Junkers

Frederick William I
canton system
Frederick II
Silesia

Map Exercises

1. Study the map on pp. 230–231, "The Growth of Prussia 1415–1918," and the accompanying caption. What general observations may be made about the growth of Prussia since 1415? What territorial changes took place between 1415 and 1688? Of what significance was Frederick II's conquest of Silesia? What general observation may be made about the geographical orientation of Prussia before and after 1815?
2. Can you locate each of the places mentioned in Section 25?

26. The "Westernizing" of Russia

Study Questions

1. Describe Russia before Peter the Great's accession to the throne. Why had Russia not shared more fully in European developments? How was this fact reflected in prevailing social conditions?
2. In what ways did changes in Russia between the time of Ivan the Terrible and the accession of Peter the Great resemble developments in other parts of Europe?
3. What was happening to the peasantry in seventeenth-century Russia? Describe peasant reactions to (a) economic changes, (b) religious changes.
4. Discuss the tempo, nature, and results of Peter the Great's internal reforms, with special attention to (a) the church, (b) the army, (c) a new capital, (d) economic policies, (e) administrative reforms.
5. How would you characterize Peter the Great's foreign policy? What territory did he win for Russia?
6. How would you assess the significance of Peter the Great in the history of Russia?

Key Discussion Sentences

Although Russia in the seventeenth century reflected its long estrangement from Europe, it was European in some of its fundamental social institutions.

Without Peter, Russia would have developed its European connections more gradually. Peter, through his tempo and methods, made the process a social revolution.

The peasant masses remained apart, egregiously exploited, never sharing in any comparable way in the Europeanized civilization.

Peter's whole system of centralized absolutism, while in form resembling that of the West, was in fact significantly different.

Peter the Great's foreign policy from the beginning was in part "defensive" and in part "expansionist."

Identifications

Mongol invasions	battle of Narva	Stephen Razin
Ivan the Terrible	Time of Troubles	Old Believers
Procurator of the Holy Synod	Michael Romanov	*gubernii*
	battle of Poltava	"state service"
"windows on the West"	rebellion of the *streltsi*	Alexis
	St. Petersburg	

Map Exercises

1. Study the map on pp. 242–243, "The Growth of Russia in the West." What general observations may be made about the westward expansion of Russia since 1462? Compare Muscovy in 1462 with (a) Russia at the beginning of Peter the Great's reign and (b) Russia at the end of Peter the Great's reign.
2. Can you locate each of the places mentioned in Section 26?

27. The Partitions of Poland

Study Questions

1. How did Austrian and Prussian concern about Russian strength in eastern Europe, and about the balance of power, lead to the first partition of Poland? What did each of the three powers gain?
2. What effect did the partition have on the Poles? Why did they not develop a more effective national resistance?

Key Discussion Sentences

Poland fell into ever deeper anarchy and confusion in the eighteenth century and was finally absorbed by its expanding neighbors.

The factor that saved the Turkish empire and condemned Poland in 1772 was the play of the European balance of power.

Identifications

John Sobieski	treaty of Kuchuk	Galicia
War of the Polish Suc- cession	Kainarji	West Prussia

Map Exercises

1. Study the map on p. 248, "Poland Since the Eighteenth Century," and the accompanying caption. What general observations may be made about Poland and the Polish boundaries before and since the eighteenth century? What observations may be made about Poland after World War II?
2. What territory did Russia, Austria, and Prussia each gain in the first partition of Poland?

GENERAL ESSAY QUESTIONS FOR CHAPTER V

1. From the mid-seventeenth century to the mid-eighteenth century three strong powers emerged and expanded in eastern Europe: Austria, Prussia, and Russia. Discuss the major steps in the evolution of each of these states, giving special consideration to (a) geographic and economic factors, (b) territorial expansion, (c) the role of individual rulers, (d) foreign policy and war. What common features do you see in the history of the three powers during these years?
2. Describe the major steps in the evolution of Russia from about 1100 through the reign of Peter the Great (1682–1725). How did the changes in Russia differ from and how did they resemble developments in western Europe during these years? Is it appropriate to speak of the "westernizing" of Russia?
3. By the early part of the eighteenth century what major political, economic, and social differences may be noted between Europe west of the "Elbe-Trieste line" and Europe east of that line?

GENERAL DISCUSSION PASSAGES FOR CHAPTER V

A line running from the mouth of the Elbe River into central Germany and down to Trieste represents one of the most important sociological boundaries in the history of modern Europe. (p. 213, map caption)

The states that insisted with such obstinacy on their liberties with respect to central authority gave few liberties to their subjects. (p. 215)

The history of the world would have been different had the Poland of the seventeenth century held together. (p. 219)

In later years some tended to romanticize unduly the old Danubian monarchy, noting that it had at least the merit of holding many discordant peoples together. (p. 224)

The Swedes in time proved themselves exceptional among European peoples in not harping on their former greatness. They successfully and peaceably made the transition from the role of a great power to that of a small one. (p. 227)

Prussia became famous for its "militarism," which may be said to exist when military needs and military values permeate all other spheres of life. (p. 227)

Prussia was unique in that, more than in any other country, the army developed a life of its own, almost independent of the life of the state, and in later generations even proved more durable than the state. (pp. 229–231)

To what extent Russia became truly European was an open question, disputed both by western Europeans and by Russians themselves. (p. 234)

Like most revolutionists since his time, Peter was aggressively secular. (p. 244)

Russian psychology, always mysterious to the West, could be explained in part by the violent paradoxes set up by rapid Europeanization. (p. 245)

Joseph Stalin was Russia's twentieth-century Peter the Great. (p. 903)

VI.
THE STRUGGLE
FOR WEALTH
AND EMPIRE
SECTIONS 28–31, pp. 250–285

28. Elite and Popular Cultures

Study Questions

1. How does one distinguish elite culture from popular culture?
2. Compare the way of life of the poor and of the well-to-do in the early eighteenth century in (a) material aspects, such as food and drink, shelter, and medical care, (b) less material aspects, such as religion, manners, and forms of entertainment. What elements were common to all classes in these years?
3. On what basis is it possible to reconstruct the mental outlook of the nonliterate and inarticulate classes?
4. What changes by the eighteenth century were sharpening the distinction between elite and popular culture?

Key Discussion Sentences

In some respects the lot of the poor was worse in the seventeenth century than in the Middle Ages.

Language was a main difference in marking off elite from popular culture.

There was much that persons of all cultures and classes shared; most important, in principle, was religion.

Between 1600 and 1700, changes took place in the attitudes of the different social classes toward witchcraft and magic, and toward popular forms of entertainment.

In the eighteenth century the gulf between elite and popular culture widened.

By the eighteenth century the elite classes were withdrawing from popular culture and the people as a whole were not yet brought into elite culture.

Identifications

elite	mountebank	*patois*
Hogarth	popular culture	Nonconformists
"carnival"	"the world turned up- side down"	

29. *The Global Economy of the Eighteenth Century*

Study Questions

1. What may be considered the most significant economic developments of the eighteenth century? What relationship do they bear to earlier economic developments?
2. Describe the role played by the British, the French, and the Dutch in the commerce of the eighteenth century. What important advantages did Britain and France enjoy over other countries?
3. What role did Asia play (a) as a market for European manufactures and (b) as a source of goods for Europeans?
4. Explain the development in America of the "plantation" economy. What role was played by the West Indies in the sugar trade? Of what importance was slave labor to the American plantation system? to the British economic system?
5. How would you assess the role played by (a) western Europe and (b) other parts of the world in the expanding world economy of the eighteenth century?
6. How did eighteenth-century economic developments affect the various social and economic classes of Europe? What was the political significance of the new wealth?
7. Why are the careers of Thomas Pitt and Jean-Joseph Laborde singled out for description? What does the painting by Oudry on p. 271 tell us about the age?

Key Discussion Sentences

In the eighteenth century the Atlantic region north of Spain became incomparably wealthier than any other part of the world.

The economic system of the eighteenth century, while it contained the seeds of later industrialism, represented the flowering of older economic institutions.

In the expanding global economy of the eighteenth century each continent played its special part.

The eighteenth century, until toward the end of the century, was an age both of commercial expansion and of social stability.

Identifications

domestic system   East India Companies   plantation economy
mercantilism

Map Exercise

1. Study the maps on pp. 196 and 284 and explain the part played by each of
   the following in the global economy of the eighteenth century: Africa, the
   East Indies, India, China, the West Indies, central Europe, and eastern
   Europe.

30. *Western Europe After Utrecht, 1713–1740*

Study Questions

1. Why may it be said that "parallel" developments were taking place in France
   and Britain in the years after Utrecht?
2. Describe political developments in France under the regency of the Duke of
   Orleans. What role did the French nobility play in the eighteenth century?
3. Analyze major political changes in Great Britain in the first half of the
   eighteenth century. Of what significance was the accession of George I? the
   ministry of Robert Walpole? Discuss the movements to "undo" the settlement
   of 1688, and their results.
4. Compare and contrast the history and the consequences of the "Mississippi
   bubble" episode in France and the "South Sea bubble" episode in England.

Key Discussion Sentences

The development of Britain and France in the years after Utrecht was in some
ways surprisingly parallel.

The eighteenth century, for France, was an age of aristocratic resurgence.

The Whigs in England could not tolerate a return of the Stuarts.

The "South Sea bubble" in England and the "Mississippi bubble" in France
both had important long-range effects.

Walpole has been called the first prime minister and the architect of cabinet
government.

Identifications

Duke of Orleans   John Law   Cardinal Fleury
the Regency   "Mississippi bubble"   George I
Whigs   Jacobites   Robert Walpole
Tories   the "Fifteen"   "Bubble Act"
Non-Jurors   the "Forty-five"   War of Jenkins' Ear
"James III"   "South Sea bubble"

31. *The Great War of the Mid-Eighteenth Century: The Peace of Paris, 1763*

Study Questions

1. What principal issues were involved in both the War of the Austrian Succession and the Seven Years' War?
2. How did warfare in the eighteenth century compare to earlier wars? to later wars?
3. In what sense was the War of the Austrian Succession a German civil struggle? a conflict between Bourbons and Habsburgs? How did the fighting overseas affect the situation in Europe? What were the major terms of the peace settlement?
4. Why may the reversal of alliances of 1756 be called a Diplomatic Revolution?
5. Describe the nature and outcome of the Seven Years' War (a) in Europe, (b) as a colonial and naval struggle between France and Britain, (c) in India. What were the stakes in this struggle?
6. Summarize and evaluate the major provisions of the treaty of Paris. In what sense was the year 1763 a ''memorable turning point''?

Key Discussion Sentences

The War of the Austrian Succession (1740–1748) and the Seven Years' War (1756–1763) were really one.

In the War of the Austrian Succession, British victories in America and on the seas tilted the balance.

In the Seven Years' War, though it was a continuation of the preceding war, the belligerents changed partners.

William Pitt subsidized Frederick of Prussia to fight in Europe so that England, as he put it, might win an empire on the plains of Germany.

The treaties of Paris and Hubertusburg made the year 1763 a memorable turning point for Europe, for America, and for India.

Identifications

Frederick II
Maria Theresa
Count Kaunitz
Pragmatic Sanction
treaty of
   Aix-la-Chapelle
Diplomatic Revolution
   of 1756

Peter III
William Pitt
Aurungzeb
Dupleix
''miracle of the house
   of Brandenburg''
peace of Hubertusburg
''Black Hole of Cal-
   cutta''

Robert Clive
French and Indian
   Wars
battle of Plassey
treaty of Paris of 1763

Map Exercises

1. Study the map on p. 284, "The World in 1763." What did the British gain by the peace settlement of 1763? What overseas territories did the French retain? What were the principal territorial changes in Europe? What general observations may be made about the peace settlement?
2. Can you locate each of the places mentioned in Section 31?

GENERAL ESSAY QUESTIONS FOR CHAPTER VI

1. How did the global economy of the eighteenth century build upon earlier economic developments? What special advances in commerce and industry took place in this century?
2. Discuss some of the social and cultural consequences of the growing wealth of western Europe. How did this growing wealth manifest itself, particularly in France and Great Britain? In what ways were elite culture and popular culture drawing apart in the seventeenth and eighteenth centuries?
3. In what sense did the "great war of the mid-eighteenth century" reflect the struggle between France and Great Britain for economic, colonial, and naval supremacy? What issues on the European continent blended with this rivalry? How did the settlement of 1763 resolve these issues?

GENERAL DISCUSSION PASSAGES FOR CHAPTER VI

The new wealth resulted from new scientific and technical knowledge, which in turn it helped to produce. The two together, more wealth and more knowledge, helped to form one of the most far-reaching ideas of modern times, the idea of progress, which retained its force well into the twentieth century. (p. 250)

Some philologists have said that no form of speech is "better" than another. But facility in the national language was a sign of elite culture and gave access to at least certain segments of the elite culture, as it continues to do today. (pp. 251–252)

Since it was so largely oral, and left so few written records, popular culture is difficult for historians to reconstruct, although it made up the daily lives, interests, and activities of the great majority in all countries. (p. 252)

What we read as history, in this as in most other books, is mostly an account of the work of a select few, either of power-wielders, decision-makers, and innovators whose actions nevertheless affected whole peoples, or of writers and thinkers whose ideas appealed to a limited audience. (p. 252)

Until toward the end of the eighteenth century the various propertied interests worked harmoniously together, and the unpropertied classes, the vast majority of the population, could influence the government only by riot and tumult. The period, though one of commercial expansion, was an age of considerable social stability in western Europe. (p. 263)

For most of the eighteenth century, war was between governments, not between whole peoples. It was fought for power, prestige, or calculated practical interests, not for ideologies, moral principles, world conquest, national survival, or ways of life. (p. 274)

Never was war so harmless, certainly not in the religious wars of earlier times, or in the national wars initiated later. (pp. 274–275)

VII.
THE SCIENTIFIC VIEW OF THE WORLD
SECTIONS 32–35, pp. 286–313

32. Prophets of a Scientific Civilization: Bacon and Descartes

Study Questions

1. Why is the history of science an important part of modern history?
2. In what sense did science become "modern" in the seventeenth century?
3. How did Francis Bacon and René Descartes attack earlier methods of seeking knowledge? What did they expect to be the results of the scientific method?
4. Explain the nature of Bacon's "inductive" method. What was his major weakness as a scientist?
5. Describe Descartes' contributions to mathematics. What is meant by Descartes' method of "systematic doubt"? by "Cartesian dualism"?

Key Discussion Sentences

The seventeenth century has been called the century of genius.

The scientific revolution of the seventeenth century had repercussions far beyond the realm of pure science.

Bacon and Descartes helped develop the scientific method and emphasized the use of scientific knowledge for practical purposes.

Identifications

deductive method
inductive method
empiricism
cogito ergo sum

Leonardo da Vinci
Montaigne
Instauratio Magna
Novum Organum

The Advancement of Learning
The New Atlantis
Discourse on Method

33. *The Road to Newton: The Law of Universal Gravitation*

Study Questions

1. Compare the Ptolemaic conception of the universe with that of Copernicus. How did Kepler further develop the Copernican theory?
2. What did Galileo's observations tell him about the nature of the heavenly bodies? Why were these views upsetting to contemporaries?
3. How did Newton build upon the work of his predecessors? What is described as his supreme achievement?
4. What advances were made in the practical and applied sciences in the seventeenth and eighteenth centuries? In what sense was the study of science becoming institutionalized?
5. Discuss the impact of the scientific revolution on the "world of thought." What were the implications of the scientific discoveries for traditional religious beliefs? for political theory and society?
6. How does the painting of the Dutch scientific scholar on p. 292 illustrate the intellectual activities of the age?

Key Discussion Sentences

It was in physics and astronomy that the most astonishing scientific revolution of the seventeenth century took place.

Natural science went along with practical invention.

The Newtonian system led to intellectual humility and to intellectual self-confidence.

The physical universe revealed by science became a model on which many thinkers hoped to refashion human society.

The revolution accomplished from Copernicus to Newton has been called the greatest spiritual adjustment that modern civilization has had to make.

Identifications

Vesalius	Galileo	Galileo's laws of mov-
William Harvey	Sir Isaac Newton	ing bodies
Leeuwenhoek	heliocentric theory	*Mathematical*
Nicholas Copernicus	*On the Revolutions of*	*Principles of Natural*
Tycho Brahe	*the Heavenly Orbs*	*Philosophy*
John Kepler		

34. New Knowledge of Man and Society

Study Questions

1. What impact did knowledge of other parts of the world have on Europe and on European thought? How did this new knowledge contribute to "skepticism"?
2. Describe the new sense of evidence that appeared in this age. How did it reveal itself in law? How did it help end the witchcraft persecutions?
3. How was the new sense of evidence reflected (a) in historical scholarship, (b) in religious scholarship?
4. Explain the significance of John Locke's writings (a) on religion and religious toleration and (b) on the nature of learning and knowledge. What were the implications of his views for social action?

Key Discussion Sentences

The influence of Europe on other parts of the world and the counterinfluence of the rest of the world upon Europe were both important.

When the variety of human manners and customs was understood, a new sense of the relative nature of social institutions emerged.

The new views of humanity and of nature were beginning to have a deep impact upon the old certainties of European life, and particularly upon Christianity.

The most profoundly disturbing of all thinkers of the age was Baruch Spinoza.

John Locke summarized in his writings many of the intellectual trends of his lifetime and exerted a strong influence on the future.

Identifications

Pierre Bayle	paleography	*Reasonableness of*
Edmund Halley	numismatics	*Christianity*
Jean Mabillon	"chronology"	*Essay Concerning*
Archbishop James	Gregorian calendar	*the Human*
Usher	Biblical criticism	*Understanding*
Richard Simon	*Letter on Toleration*	

Map Exercise

1. Study the maps on pp. 302–303, "The Growth of Geographical Knowledge." What do the four panels reveal about advances in geographical knowledge from the sixteenth to the eighteenth century?

35. *Political Theory: The School of Natural Law*

Study Questions

1. In what sense did Machiavelli attempt to adopt a scientific view in *The Prince*? In what way was his analysis not scientific?
2. What is meant by "natural law"? "natural right"? How, according to natural law philosophy, was natural law to be "discovered"?
3. Explain how the philosophy of natural law was used to justify both absolutist and constitutional government in the seventeenth century. Compare and contrast the political theories of Thomas Hobbes and John Locke.
4. How did Locke justify the English Revolution of 1688? How did he make it seem modern and forward-looking?

Key Discussion Sentences

The seventeenth century was the classic age of the philosophy of natural right and of natural law.

On the basis of natural law some thinkers tried to create international law.

Locke's writings converted the English Revolution of 1688 into an event of universal meaning.

Both Locke and Hobbes, and the whole school of natural law, held that government was based on a kind of contract.

Identifications

The Prince	Samuel Pufendorf	*Two Treatises of*
Hugo Grotius	*Leviathan*	*Government*

GENERAL ESSAY QUESTIONS FOR CHAPTER VII

1. Why may the seventeenth century be called the century of genius? Explain with reference to (a) advances in science and scientific thought, (b) new ways of thinking about human beings, society, and politics, (c) new geographical knowledge, (d) changed ideas about religion and the universe.
2. Why did the scientific revolution of the seventeenth and eighteenth centuries call for a spiritual adjustment and a questioning of traditional beliefs? How did it compel contemporaries to reassess attitudes derived from (a) the Middle Ages, (b) the Renaissance, (c) the Reformation?
3. How did ideas derived from science carry over into ideas of natural law and natural rights?

GENERAL DISCUSSION PASSAGES FOR CHAPTER VII

To have a humanistic understanding of the powers of the human mind, one must sense the importance of science—as of philosophy, literature, or the arts. Science, purely as a form of thought, represents one of the supreme achievements of the human mind. (p. 287)

Ideas have a way of passing over from science into other domains of thought. Many people today, for example, are influenced by ideas which they believe to be those of Darwin, Freud, or Einstein—they talk of evolution, repression, or relativity, without necessarily knowing much about them. (p. 287)

In the coming together of knowledge and power arose the far-reaching modern idea of progress. And with it arose many modern problems, since the power given by scientific knowledge can be used for either good or evil. (p. 290)

For Bayle, as for Montaigne, no opinion was worth burning your neighbor for. (p. 302)

History, like law, depends on the finding and using of evidence. The historian and the judge must answer the same kind of question—did such-and-such really occur? (p. 303)

A common system of dating events for the world's peoples is of more importance than may be at first thought. It is a great aid to thinking of human history as an interconnected whole. (p. 305)

Locke's environmentalist philosophy became fundamental to liberal reform in later years. If human evil was due to the imperfections of social institutions, the improvement of human society would improve human behavior. (p. 307)

Political theory can never be strictly scientific. Science deals with what exists or has existed. It does not tell what ought to exist. But it is impossible in human affairs to escape the word "ought." (p. 307)

Machiavelli observed that successful rulers behaved as if holding or increasing power were their only object and that they regarded all else as means to that end. Governments, in fact, continued to behave for the most part as Machiavelli said. (p. 308)

The idea of natural law has underlain a good deal of modern democratic development, and its decline has been closely connected with many of the troubles of contemporary times. (p. 308)

Under natural law philosophy, man is considered to be a rational animal. And all human beings are assumed to have, at least potentially and when more enlightened, the same powers of reason and understanding. (p. 309)

By the twentieth century it was widely thought that the human mind was not essentially rational but was motivated by drives or urges or instincts, and that human differences were so fundamental that people of different nationalities or classes could never expect to see things in the same way. When this happened, the older philosophy of natural law lost its hold. (p. 309)

Events in England, as explained by Locke, and as seen through his eyes in many countries, including England and its colonies, launched into the mainstream of modern history the superb tradition of constitutional government, which has been one of the main themes in the history of the modern world ever since. (p. 301)

By 1700 some beliefs that were to be characteristic of modern times had clearly taken form, notably a faith in science, in human reason, in natural human rights, and in progress. These ideas were eventually to revolutionize Europe, America, and the world. They were also, in subsequent years, to be modified, amended, challenged, and even denied. But they are still very much alive today. (p. 313)

VIII.
THE AGE OF
ENLIGHTENMENT
SECTIONS 36–40, pp. 314–360

36. The Philosophes—And Others

Study Questions

1. From what sources was the thought of the Enlightenment drawn? What elements are suggested as basic to the spirit of the Enlightenment? Of what significance was the idea of progress?
2. What currents of thought and practice contradictory to Enlightenment attitudes were also prevalent in this age? How did these differences reflect the gap between popular and elite culture?
3. What general observations may be made about the philosophes and the audience for whom they wrote? What effect did censorship have upon the writings of the day?
4. What contributions to the Enlightenment were made by the *Encyclopédie*? the Physiocrats? Adam Smith?
5. Discuss and compare the contributions made to the thought of the Enlightenment by (a) Montesquieu, (b) Voltaire, (c) Rousseau.
6. Explain the attitudes held by thinkers of the Enlightenment toward (a) religion and the churches, (b) the function of the state, (c) the problem of liberty.

Key Discussion Sentences

The spirit of the eighteenth-century Enlightenment was drawn from the scientific and intellectual revolution of the seventeenth century.

The currents of thought in the eighteenth century were divergent and inconsistent, but there was a general belief in reason, science, civilization, and progress.

Although the thought of the Enlightenment was secular, the first half of the eighteenth century was also a time of continuing religious fervor for many, and even of interest in the mysterious.

Although the French word *philosophe* means philosopher, it is used to denote a group of writers who were not philosophers in the technical sense of the word.

For Voltaire and most philosophes the ideal form of government approached that of enlightened despotism.

Rousseau was probably the most profound writer of the age and certainly the most permanently influential.

Identifications

Ancients and Moderns
The Messiah
Pietism
John Wesley
Mesmer
Freemasonry
Illuminati
philosophes
Encyclopedists
Helvetius
Mme. de Geoffrin
Sophie Condorcet
Mme. de Staël

Écrasez l'infâme
Decline and Fall of the
    Roman Empire
The Spirit of Laws
Philosophical Letters
    on the English
Age of Louis XIV
Calas affair
La Barre episode
Diderot
Sketch of the Progress
    of the Human Mind
Essai sur les moeurs

Arts and Sciences
Origins of Inequality
    Among Men
Social Contract
Considerations on
    Poland
Émile
Physiocrats
laissez-faire
Political Arithmetic
Wealth of Nations
Condorcet

37. *Enlightened Despotism: France, Austria, Prussia*

Study Questions

1. What characteristics distinguished the enlightened despots from earlier monarchs? How did the wars of the mid-eighteenth century contribute to enlightened despotism?
2. Assess the successes and failures of enlightened despotism in France. How did the attempted abolition of the parlements illustrate its weaknesses?
3. Compare the changes introduced by Maria Theresa and by Joseph II in the Austrian Empire. Would you characterize both as enlightened despots?
4. Discuss the nature and results of enlightened despotism in Prussia under Frederick the Great. Of what special importance was the stratification of Prussian society?

Key Discussion Sentences

The typical enlightened despots differed from their "unenlightened" predecessors mainly in attitude and tempo.

The typical enlightened despot set out to reform and reconstruct the state in order to make it more rational and more uniform.

In France, enlightened despotism had less success than elsewhere.

Maria Theresa proceeded with caution in her reforms for Austria.

Joseph II was a pure representative of the Age of Enlightenment, and it is in his brief reign of ten years that the character and limitations of enlightened despotism can best be seen.

Frederick the Great's fame as an enlightened despot rested more on his intellectual achievements than on any sweeping reforms in Prussia.

Identifications

après moi le déluge	*corvée*	Febronianism
taille	Maria Theresa	the ''revolutionary
''free gift''	Joseph II	emperor''
''Maupeou parlements''	Leopold II	''hereditary subjects''
Turgot	cameralism	

38. *Enlightened Despotism: Russia*

Study Questions

1. How did the intellectual currents of the Enlightenment affect Russia?
2. Describe the personality and personal qualities of Catherine, and assess her reform program. What seems to have thwarted that program?
3. Describe Catherine's foreign policy and the territorial growth of Russia during her reign. What did Russia gain in the partitions of Poland?
4. What general observations may be made about the accomplishments, short-comings, and limitations of enlightened despotism in Europe in this age?

Key Discussion Sentences

The Enlightenment in Russia furthered the estrangement of the Russian upper classes from their own people and their own native scene.

Even at the end of her reign, Catherine continued to recognize the standards of the Enlightenment—at least as standards.

Territorially, Catherine was one of the main builders of Russia.

Enlightened despotism represented an effort to revolutionize society by authoritative action from above, but the enlightened despots reached a point beyond which they could not go.

Identifications

Legislative Commission	Catherine's "Greek	treaty of Kuchuk
Pugachev rebellion	project"	Kainarji
muzhik	partitions of Poland	"Potemkin villages"
the Eastern Question		

Map Exercises

1. Study the map on p. 242, "The Growth of Russia in the West," and indicate the geographical boundaries of Russia before and after the reign of Catherine the Great.
2. Study the map on p. 248, "Poland Since the Eighteenth Century." Describe the territory gained by Russia, Prussia, and Austria in each of the three partitions of Poland. (See also map on p. 328, "Europe, 1740.")

39. New Stirrings: The British Reform Movement

Study Questions

1. What observations may be made about political developments in the European world beginning about 1760? What arguments may be advanced for and against the thesis that the revolutionary movements of the age were aspects of "one great revolutionary wave"?
2. What common demands were raised by the revolutionary movements of the age? Which could be characterized as "democratic" and which as not?
3. How did the Enlightenment in Britain differ from the Enlightenment on the Continent?
4. Why was there political and social dissent in England? What special factors served as barriers to reform?
5. What relationship developed between reformers in England and the American colonials?
6. How was the trend toward centralization in the British Empire in this age reflected in developments in Scotland? in Ireland? in India?
7. How do the portraits by Gainsborough and Copley (pp. 346 and 352) illustrate social classes in the eighteenth-century Atlantic world?

Key Discussion Sentences

An important era of revolutionary disturbance opened about 1760 that did not end until after the revolutions of 1848.

Even if the reform movements are not viewed as part of a single great revolutionary wave, the revolutionaries or reformers shared much in common.

Reform movements in this age were both democratic and undemocratic.

The middle classes were the great beneficiaries of this revolutionary age.

Although Parliament was supreme in England, and constitutional questions were apparently settled after 1688, there were undercurrents of discontent.

The reform movement in England was closely associated with events in America.

The trend in the British world in the eighteenth century was toward a centralization of the empire under the authority of Parliament.

Identifications

age of the ''Atlantic Revolution''	Tory	''placemen''
age of the ''Democratic Revolution''	Dissenters	Act of Union of 1801
	''commonwealthmen''	Warren Hastings
''patriot king''	John Wilkes	India Acts of 1773 and
''king's friends''	John Cartwright	1784
	Edmund Burke	

40. *The American Revolution*

Study Questions

1. How would you characterize the behavior and attitudes of the American colonists in the years preceding the American Revolution?
2. How did events connected with the East India Company lead to the ''Boston tea party''? What retaliatory measures did the British government take?
3. How did the War of American Independence become part of the European struggle for empire?
4. How did the principles announced in the Declaration of Independence reflect the thought of the Enlightenment?
5. What advances toward democratic equality were made in connection with the American Revolution? What limitations on these advances should be pointed out?
6. Discuss the political consequences of the American Revolution for Europe and the world. How did it affect older European political attitudes?

Key Discussion Sentences

Disregard of law was commonplace in the eighteenth century, yet the British Americans were possibly the least law-abiding of all the more civilized European peoples.

It was the participation of the French army and fleet that made possible the defeat of the British.

The upheaval in America was a revolution as well as a war for independence.

In the new states democratic equality made many advances.

The democratic advances of the American Revolution were subject to limitations.

The Americans drew heavily on Locke and on ideas that went back to the Puritan Revolution.

The American Revolution made the older ideas of constitutionalism, federalism, and limited government, once associated with feudalism and aristocracy, progressive and democratic.

Identifications

Revenue Act of 1764	*Common Sense*	federalism
Stamp Act	"Intolerable Acts"	Articles of
"Townshend duties"	Continental Congresses	Confederation
"virtual	Thomas Paine	Northwest Ordinance
representation"	treaty of 1783	
Quebec Act	American "Tories"	

GENERAL ESSAY QUESTIONS FOR CHAPTER VIII

1. What relationships do you see between the seventeenth-century "age of genius" and the eighteenth-century "Age of Enlightenment"? How did the philosophes reflect the skeptical, rational, and scientific spirit of both centuries?
2. Discuss the main currents of Enlightenment thought with respect to (a) science, (b) government, (c) economic policies, (d) religion, (e) education. Why would the attitudes of the age reinforce faith in the idea of progress?
3. How were the ideas of the Enlightenment applied in their respective countries by (a) enlightened monarchs on the Continent, (b) the British reform movement, (c) the American Revolutionists? In what sense did the American Revolution transform older ideas of constitutionalism, federalism, and limited government?

GENERAL DISCUSSION PASSAGES FOR CHAPTER VIII

Never has there been an age so skeptical toward tradition, so confident in the powers of human reason and of science, so firmly convinced of the regularity and harmony of nature, and so deeply imbued with the sense of civilization's advance and progress. (p. 315)

The idea of progress is often said to be the dominant or characteristic idea of European civilization from the seventeenth century to the twentieth century. It is a belief, a kind of nonreligious faith, that the conditions of human life become better as time goes on, that in general each generation is better off than its predecessors and will contribute by its labors to an even better life for generations to come, and that in the long run all humanity will share in the same advance. (p. 315)

The Ancients held that the works of the Greeks and Romans had never been surpassed. The Moderns, pointing to science, art, literature, and invention, declared that their own time was the best, that it was natural to do better than the Ancients because they came later and built upon their predecessors' achievements. (p. 315)

The symbol of God which occurred to people of scientific view in the Age of Enlightenment was that of Watchmaker. (p. 315)

The Physiocrats were the first to use the term *laissez-faire* ("let them do as they see fit") as a principle of economic activity. (p. 324)

Adam Smith's purpose, like that of the Physiocrats, was to increase the national wealth by the reduction of barriers that hindered its growth. The motivation for all production and exchange was to be the self-interest of the participants. The system was morally justified since it would ultimately produce a maximum both of freedom and of abundance. (pp. 324–325)

If the Enlightenment thinkers believed that the main agency of progress was the state, they were not nationalists in any later sense of the word. They believed in the unity of mankind under a natural law of right and reason. In this they carried over the classical and Christian outlook in a secular way. (p. 326)

In England there was general contentment with the arrangements that followed the Revolution of 1688—it has often been remarked that nothing is so conservative as a successful revolution. (p. 344)

In the new states democratic equality made many advances. But the democratic advances of the American Revolution long applied only to white males of European origin. To apply the principles of liberty and equality without regard to race or sex in the age of the American Revolution was beyond the powers of Americans at the time. (p. 356)

Americans came to believe, more than any other people, that governments should possess limited powers and operate only within the terms of a fixed and written constitutional document. (p. 357)

Federalism, or the allocation of power between central and outlying governments, went along with the idea of written constitutions as a principal offering of Americans to the world. (p. 358)

The United States, as its later history was to show, bore a heavy load of inherited burdens and unsolved problems, especially racial. But in a general way, until new revolutionary movements set in a century later, America stood as a kind of utopia for the common man. (p. 360)

IX.
THE FRENCH REVOLUTION
SECTIONS 41–46, pp. 361–402
PICTURE ESSAY, pp. 403–415

41. Backgrounds

Study Questions

1. In what ways did the legal division of society under the Old Regime fail to reflect actual political and social conditions in France? What observations may be made about the existing property system?
2. Describe the changes taking place in both the nobility and the bourgeoisie prior to the Revolution. How did these changes contribute to the Revolution?
3. What features of the agrarian and manorial system of the Old Regime were survivals of the feudal age? What is meant by the "feudal reaction" of the eighteenth century? What effect did it have on the peasants?
4. How did the political unity of France contribute to the Revolution?
5. Discuss the role played by the church in the Old Regime.
6. Describe the condition of people in the Third Estate below the commercial and professional families. What do the paintings by David and Millet (pp. 382 and 386) reveal about the lower classes in France?

Key Discussion Sentences

The three legal estates in French society under the Old Regime bore little relationship to political, social, and economic actualities.

The Revolution was the collision of two moving objects, a rising aristocracy and a rising bourgeoisie.

The political unity of France was a fundamental prerequisite, and even a cause, of the Revolution.

The Revolution was to revolutionize the law of property by establishing the free and direct ownership of land.

Identifications

Old Regime	taille	*banalités*
First, Second, and	tithe	"eminent property"
Third Estates	*métayer*	rights
Estates-General	"hunting rights"	

42. *The Revolution and the Reorganization of France*

Study Questions

1. How did the financial crisis facing the French government lead to revolution?
2. What special circumstances created hardship for the lower classes? What manifestations of unrest appeared in the city? in the countryside? How did these events affect the National Assembly?
3. What major principles were announced in the Declaration of the Rights of Man and Citizen? Of what significance was the Declaration to be? What might be said of the rights of women in the Revolutionary era?
4. How did the Constituent Assembly overhaul the institutions of the Old Regime?
5. Assess the machinery of government established by the Constitution of 1791.
6. Describe the legislation introduced by the Constituent Assembly with respect to (a) public finances, (b) church lands, (c) guilds and other labor organizations.
7. Discuss the nature and the consequences of the religious measures adopted by the Constituent Assembly.

Key Discussion Sentences

Although France was prosperous in 1789, the government treasury was empty.

The nobility forced the summoning of the Estates-General and in this way initiated the Revolution.

Short-run conditions in 1789 were bad.

The Great Fear became part of a general agrarian insurrection. The peasants intended to destroy the manorial regime by force.

The Declaration of the Rights of Man and Citizen affirmed the principles of the new society.

The Constituent Assembly went about its work of simultaneously governing the country, devising a constitution, and destroying in detail the institutions of the Old Regime.

The attitude of Louis XVI greatly disoriented the Revolution.

All the new machinery of state was by no means democratic.

The Civil Constitution of the Clergy has been called the greatest tactical blunder of the Revolution.

Identifications

Calonne
Loménie de Brienne
What Is the Third Estate?
National Assembly
"active" and "passive" citizens
The Rights of Man
The Rights of Woman
Tennis Court Oath

capture of the Bastille
Great Fear of 1789
"night of August 4"
Declaration of the Rights of Man and Citizen
"electors"
assignats
Mary Wollstonecraft
"patriots"

Count of Artois
march on Versailles
Jacobin
Constitution of 1791
"flight to Varennes"
Le Chapelier law
nonjuring clergy
Olympe de Gouges

43. The Revolution and Europe: The War and the "Second" Revolution, 1792

Study Questions

1. Describe the general impact of the Revolution upon its age. What different interpretations did contemporaries give to the events taking place? What position was taken by Burke?
2. What were the reactions of the various European governments to the revolutionary events in France?
3. How did the Declaration of Pillnitz affect developments in France? Why did various groups in France favor war?
4. Why were peasants and urban workers dissatisfied with the course of the Revolution so far?
5. Why may the insurrection of August 10, 1792, be called the "second" French Revolution?

Key Discussion Sentences

In 1789, pro-French and pro-revolutionary groups appeared all over Europe, but in all countries there were also enemies of the Revolution.

The Declaration of Pillnitz rested on a famous "if."

The Girondins became the party of international revolution.

When the war came, the lower classes rallied to the Revolution but not to the revolutionary government in power.

In the summer of 1792, great masses of the French people burst out in a passion of nationalist and patriotic excitement.

Identifications

Reflections on the Revo-lution in France	Leopold II	*Marseillaise*
émigrés	Girondins	storming of the
Count of Artois	Mme. Roland	Tuileries
Miranda	Francis II	"September
	Brunswick Manifesto	massacres"
		William Pitt

44. The Emergency Republic, 1792–1795: The Terror

Study Questions

1. What relationship was there between French military expansion and the spread of the Revolution? How did the European powers resist? What factors weakened the coalition fighting France?
2. Explain the political division that developed inside the Convention. What policies did the Mountain represent?
3. Of what significance was the execution of the king? the insurrection of May 31, 1793?
4. Discuss the problems and difficulties faced by the Convention in the spring of 1793. What program did it follow? With what results?
5. How may the loss of lives in "the Terror" be distinguished from the loss of lives in other ways during the Revolution?
6. Describe the events and significance of 9 Thermidor. What developments took place in the months that followed?

Key Discussion Sentences

The militancy and activism of the sans-culottes pressed the Revolution forward.

After the insurrection of May 1793, the Mountain ruled in the Convention but the Convention itself ruled very little.

Robespierre is one of the most argued about and least understood men of modern times.

To repress the counterrevolution, the Convention set up what is popularly known as the "Reign of Terror."

The triumphant element after Thermidor was the bourgeois class.

Identifications

National Convention
battle of Valmy
sans-culottes
Dumouriez
revolt of the Vendée
"federalist" rebellions
enragés
"Reign of Terror"
Maximilien Robespierre

Committee of General
   Security
Committee of Public
   Safety
levée en masse
"general maximum"
Constitution of 1793
Ventôse laws of March
   1794

Hébertists
Dechristianization
Revolutionary calendar
"Worship of the
   Supreme Being"
"Thermidorian
   reaction"
insurrection of Prairial

45. The Constitutional Republic: The Directory, 1795–1799

Study Questions

1. How would you characterize the nature of the Directory? From what sources did it face opposition?
2. Why might Napoleon Bonaparte have been disturbed by the elections of 1797? Describe Bonaparte's background, career, and accomplishments to this point.
3. How did the coup d'état of Fructidor affect the peace negotiations going on? Of what significance was the peace treaty that was signed?
4. Discuss the military and political circumstances that prepared the way for Bonaparte's seizure of power.

Key Discussion Sentences

The Directory had enemies to both right and left.

The treaty of Campo Formio with Austria represented a victory for Bonaparte's ideas.

For those who sought "confidence from below, authority from above" Bonaparte seemed the answer.

Identifications

Directory
Constitution of 1795
"perpetuals"
"Louis XVIII"
Declaration of Verona

"Gracchus" Babeuf
General Augereau
treaty of Campo
   Formio
Second Coalition

battle of the Nile (or
   Aboukir)
Sieyès
coup d'état of Brumaire

Map Exercise

1. Study the map on p. 396, "The French Republic and Its Satellites, 1798–1799." What direct annexations did the Republic make? List the chief satellite republics. What did the treaty of Campo Formio provide with respect to the German states?

46. *The Authoritarian Republic: The Consulate, 1799–1804*

PICTURE ESSAY: A REVOLUTIONARY ERA (pp. 403–415)

Study Questions

1. Evaluate the personality, talents, and political ideas of Bonaparte.
2. What kind of governmental machinery was set up under the Consulate? Where did real authority reside?
3. Describe and evaluate the significance of the major reforms introduced by Bonaparte (a) in law and administration, (b) in public finance and taxation, (c) in church-state relations.
4. How would you summarize the major accomplishments of the Revolution by the end of the Consulate? In what ways had the Revolution strengthened France? How did the governments of Europe regard Napoleon?
5. How does the Picture Essay communicate the sense of a revolutionary era and an age of democratic revolution in both Europe and America?

Key Discussion Sentences

Bonaparte was, or seemed, just what many Frenchmen were looking for after ten years of upheaval.

Bonaparte may be thought of as the last and most eminent of the enlightened despots.

Under the Consulate the modern state took on clearer form; it was the reverse of everything feudal.

Both sides gained from the Concordat of 1801.

With the Consulate the Revolution in France was over. If its highest hopes had not been accomplished, the worst evils of the Old Regime had at least been cured.

France, no longer revolutionary at home, was revolutionary outside its borders.

Identifications

"plebiscite"	"prefect"	"careers open to
"notables"	Fouché	talent"

Council of State   Talleyrand   Bank of France
treaty of Lunéville   Concordat of 1801   Code Napoleon

GENERAL ESSAY QUESTIONS FOR CHAPTER IX

1. How did the Revolution in the years 1789–1804 replace the Old Regime in France with a more "modern" society?
2. What separate phases can be distinguished in the Revolution between 1789 and 1804? Describe (a) the principal moving forces in each phase, and (b) the accomplishments and limitations of each phase.
3. Why were the doctrines of the Revolution highly exportable? What impact did they have on the various classes of Europe? What effect did the coming of war have on the Revolution?
4. In what sense did the Revolution accelerate older trends and in what sense was it innovative?
5. What new conceptions of liberty and equality emerged from both the American and French Revolutions? How may the course of the revolution and the outcome in each be compared?
6. In what sense was Bonaparte (a) a "child of the Enlightenment and of the Revolution," (b) "the last of the enlightened despots"?

GENERAL DISCUSSION PASSAGES FOR CHAPTER IX

In 1789 France fell into revolution, and the world has never since been the same. All later revolutionary movements have looked upon it as a predecessor. (p. 361)

Under the Declaration of the Rights of Man and Citizen, liberty was defined as the freedom to do anything not injurious to others, which in turn was to be determined only by law. (p. 371)

In the phrase the "rights of man" the word "man" applied without respect to nationality, race, or sex. The Declaration of 1789 was not meant to refer to males only. But when it came to particular rights, as in voting, family law, property, and education, the Revolutionaries went no further than contemporary opinion and assigned broader political, property, and educational rights to males. (pp. 371–372)

Although few at the time argued for legal equality between the sexes, there were some voices explicitly raised for the rights of women. (p. 372)

The French Revolution was innovative in that it gave new meanings to liberty, equality, civil rights, property, and representative government. (p. 403)

The doctrines of the French Revolution, as of the American, were highly exportable: They took the form of a universal philosophy, proclaiming human rights, regardless of time or place, race or nation. (p. 378)

In all countries in the age of the French Revolution there were revolutionary or pro-French elements that were feared by their own governments. In all countries also there were people whose loyalties lay abroad. There had been no such situation since the Protestant Reformation, nor was there anything like it again until after the Russian Revolution of the twentieth century. (p. 379)

By the standards of the twentieth century, in which governments have undertaken to wipe out whole classes or races, the number who perished in the Terror, as victims of the official government repression, was not large. Yet the Terror was inhuman at best and in some places atrocious. (p. 388)

The French Republic, in falling into the hands of Napoleon Bonaparte, fell to a man of such remarkable talents as are often denominated genius. (p. 398)

Bonaparte delighted in affirming the sovereignty of the people, but to his mind the people was a sovereign, like Voltaire's God, who somehow created the world but never thereafter interfered in it. (p. 399)

The new France could tap the wealth of its citizens and put able men into position without inquiring into their origins. Every private, boasted Napoleon, carried a marshal's baton in his knapsack. (p. 402)

X.
NAPOLEONIC
EUROPE
SECTIONS 47–51, pp. 417–452

47. *The Formation of the French Imperial System*

Study Questions

1. What general observations may be made about internal changes in the European countries in the years of Napoleon's ascendancy? about the nature and motives of the governments that fought Napoleon?
2. How and why did the First Coalition against Napoleon break up? the Second Coalition?
3. Of what significance was the treaty of Amiens? How did Bonaparte's policies provoke the formation of the Third Coalition? What was its outcome?
4. Why did the attitudes and policies of Tsar Alexander I puzzle and disturb his contemporaries? In what sense may the treaty of Tilsit be considered the high point of Napoleon's success? What led to the weakening of the alliance with Alexander?
5. Explain the origins, purpose, and nature of Napoleon's Continental System. What effect did Napoleon's setbacks in Spain have on other parts of Europe?
6. In what sense was the Napoleonic empire at its height in the years 1809–1811?

Key Discussion Sentences

The French impact, though based on military success, represented more than mere forcible subjugation.

The history of the Napoleonic period would be much simpler if the European governments had merely fought to protect themselves against the aggressive French.

In 1802 Napoleon used peace, as he had war, to advance his interests—in the New World, in Italy, in Switzerland, and in Germany.

Tsar Alexander, after Napoleon himself, was the most considerable figure on the European stage in these years.

Because there was no foreseeable possibility of invading England after Trafalgar, Napoleon turned to economic warfare.

By 1810 Napoleon, the Son of the Revolution, could refer to the emperor of Austria as "my father" and was by marriage the nephew of Louis XVI.

Identifications

treaty of Amiens	Confederation of the	capitulation at Baylen
the "shame of the	Rhine	Grand Duchy of
princes"	Jena and Auerstädt	Warsaw
Ulm	Eylau	Talleyrand
Trafalgar	Friedland	Wagram
Austerlitz	treaty of Tilsit	Metternich
treaty of Pressburg	Peninsular War	

Map Exercise

1. Study the map on p. 430, "Napoleonic Germany." How did Napoleon contribute to the consolidation of the German states?

48. The Grand Empire: Spread of the Revolution

Study Questions

1. Describe the territory dominated by Napoleon at the height of his influence. (Consult also the map on p. 427.) What main divisions were there to the Napoleonic domain?
2. Explain the government and administration of the French empire and of the Grand Empire. How did Napoleon use his family as a means of rule?
3. What justification is there for considering Napoleon a reformer and a man of the Enlightenment? In what sense were the main principles of the French Revolution spread throughout Europe by Napoleon?
4. What appeal did the Napoleonic system have in Europe? To what extent was repression employed?

Key Discussion Sentences

Napoleon believed in the unity of European civilization.

Napoleon called his system "liberal" and believed in "constitutions."

Napoleon's reforms throughout Europe were directed against everything feudal.

Under Napoleon, some of the main principles of the French Revolution—with the notable exception of self-government—were introduced in all countries of the Grand Empire.

Napoleon, it seemed to Goethe, "was the expression of all that was reasonable, legitimate, and European in the revolutionary movement."

Identifications

French Empire	Civil Code	Confederation of the
Grand Empire	Illyrian Provinces	Rhine
"allied states"	Grand Duchy of	Kingdom of Westphalia
"King of Rome"	Warsaw	"Kingdom of Italy"
Pius VII		

Map Exercise

1. On the outline map of Europe show the boundaries of France in 1792, before the Revolutionary and Napoleonic wars. On the same map show at the height of Napoleon's power about 1810 the boundaries of (a) the French Empire, (b) the Grand Empire and its constituent parts, (c) the states allied with Napoleon. Indicate also the location of the most important battles of the Napoleonic era. Suggested source: *A History of the Modern World*, pp. 328 and 427.

49. The Continental System: Britain and Europe

Study Questions

1. Describe Napoleon's efforts to find a basis other than force for the unification of Europe. How did he hope to exploit existing attitudes toward Great Britain?
2. In what basic way did the British blockade and Napoleon's Continental System resemble each other? How did the United States become involved in this economic warfare? With what results?
3. Explain the objective of Napoleon's Continental System with respect to the economy of Continental Europe.
4. What were the chief reasons for the failure of the Continental System? What effect did it have as a short-range war measure?

Key Discussion Sentences

To arouse a European feeling, Napoleon worked upon the latent hostility to Great Britain.

The purpose of the Continental System, as of the British blockade, was not to keep imports out of the enemy country, but to destroy the enemy's export markets.

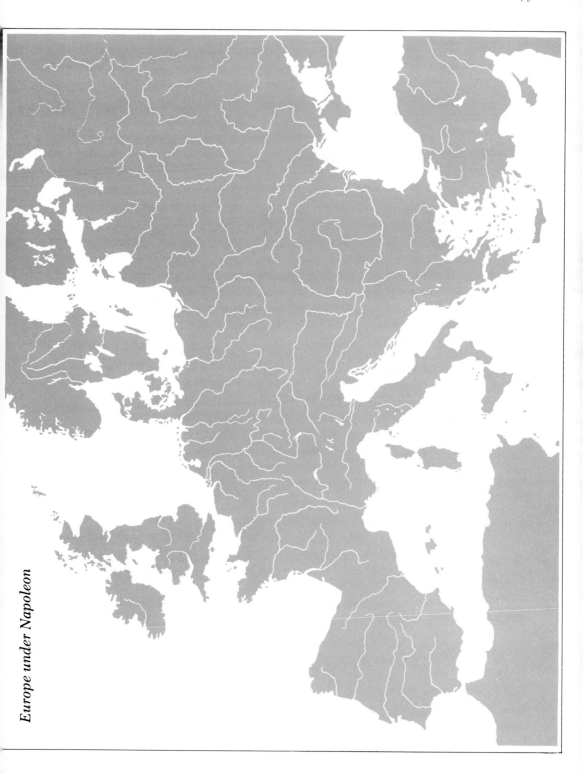

Europe under Napoleon

The Continental System was also a scheme to develop the economy of Continental Europe around France as its main center.

The Continental System was worse than a failure, for it caused widespread antagonism to the Napoleonic regime.

Identifications

"nation of   "order of council" of   Milan decree
  shopkeepers"   1807
Berlin decree

50. The National Movements: Germany

Study Questions

1. Of what significance was the Napoleonic age for the development of national-ism? What different forms did nationalist feelings take?
2. Describe the change in German national-mindedness that set in about 1780. How did the ideas emerging in Germany differ from the ideas characteristic of the Enlightenment?
3. Discuss the development of nationalist political thought in Napoleonic Germany. In what sense was it "democratic"? What manifestations of German nationalist activities appeared?
4. Describe (a) the principal aims of the army reformers in Prussia and (b) the political philosophy and reforms of Baron Stein.

Key Discussion Sentences

Nationalism developed as a movement of resistance against the forcible interna-tionalism of the Napoleonic empire.

The nationalism of the Napoleonic period was a mixture of the conservative and the liberal.

German ideas fell in with the ferment of fundamental thinking known as romanticism, which everywhere challenged the ideas of the Enlightenment.

The reform program in Prussia was aimed at strengthening Prussia for a war of liberation against Napoleon.

Identifications

Herder   *Germany in Its Deep*   *Closed Commercial*
romanticism   *Humiliation*   *State*
Volksgeist   Fichte   Gneisenau
"Father" Jahn   *Addresses to the Ger-*   Baron Stein
             man Nation   *Tugendbund*

51. *The Overthrow of Napoleon:*
The Congress of Vienna

Study Questions

1. What factors made everything go "wrong" in Napoleon's invasion of Russia in 1812? How did Europe react to Napoleon's setback in Russia?
2. To what extent did the charter of 1814 accept the changes of the Revolution and the Napoleonic era?
3. Explain the nature of the "first" Treaty of Paris. How would you summarize the issues facing Europe after the defeat of Napoleon?
4. Describe the principal territorial arrangements adopted at the Congress of Vienna. What attitudes were taken toward the peace settlement by (a) Prussia, (b) Russia, (c) Great Britain, (d) Austria? How was the dispute over Poland settled?
5. Why did so many of the French people rally to Napoleon upon his return? How did the allies react?
6. How would you evaluate the accomplishments and failures of the Peace of Vienna? Why was the settlement a disappointment to many?

Key Discussion Sentences

After Napoleon's retreat from Moscow all the anti-Napoleonic forces rushed together.

The closer the allies came to defeating Napoleon, the more they began to fear and distrust each other.

Castlereagh and Metternich, with support from Talleyrand, sought to restore a balance of power on the Continent.

The question of Poland almost brought the Congress of Vienna to disaster.

The Peace of Vienna had its strong points and its weak ones. With past issues the peace of 1815 dealt rather effectively; with future issues, not unnaturally, it was less successful.

Identifications

Borodino
retreat from Moscow
battle of Leipzig
"Frankfurt proposals"
Castlereagh
Metternich

Talleyrand
Louis XVIII
Quadruple Alliance
charter of 1814
"first" Treaty of Paris
Polish-Saxon question

"Congress Poland"
battle of Waterloo
Hundred Days
"second" Treaty of
    Paris
Holy Alliance

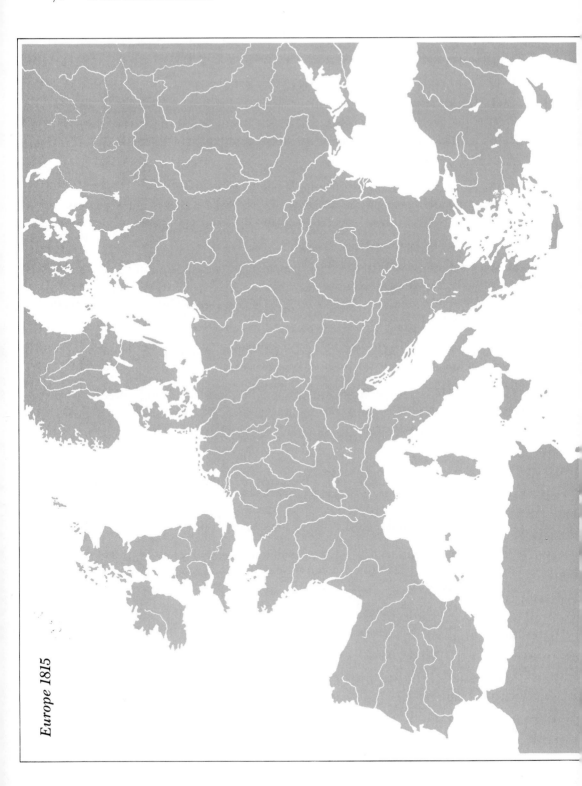

Europe 1815

Map Exercises

1. On the outline map of Europe show the European boundaries set by the Congress of Vienna in 1815. How do they compare with European boundaries in 1792? Suggested source: *A History of the Modern World*, pp. 328 and 448–449.
2. Study the maps on pp. 230–231, 242–243, and 248. (a) What was meant by the Polish-Saxon question at the Congress of Vienna? (b) What effect did the peace settlement of 1815 have upon the boundaries of both Prussia and Russia?
3. Can you locate each of the places mentioned in Section 51?

GENERAL ESSAY QUESTIONS FOR CHAPTER X

1. "Of the Napoleonic ascendancy of fifteen years two stories are to be told. One is the story of international relations, reflecting the diverse interests of the contending states of Europe. The other is the story of the internal development of the European peoples." Develop this theme, explaining also how the two stories are interrelated.
2. Explain how the reforms that originated in the French Revolution were spread throughout Europe by Napoleon. How did they strengthen the European countries? What resentments did Napoleon's rule arouse?
3. How did Napoleon's ascendancy over Europe help reinforce nationalism, political and cultural? What role did nationalism play in his downfall?
4. Discuss the foreign policy followed by Britain, Austria, Prussia, and Russia (a) in the French Revolutionary wars, 1792–1799, (b) in the Napoleonic wars, 1799–1815. How consistently was the balance-of-power idea applied?
5. Compare and evaluate the peace settlements of (a) Westphalia, 1648, (b) Utrecht, 1713–1714, (c) Paris, 1763, and (d) Vienna, 1814–1815. By what criteria may a peace settlement be assessed? How successfully did the Congress of Vienna deal with the issues it faced?

GENERAL DISCUSSION PASSAGES FOR CHAPTER X

Napoleon came nearer than anyone has ever come to imposing political unity on the European continent. (p. 417)

Whether by collaboration or resistance, Europe was transformed in the Napoleonic years. (p. 417)

Napoleon carried over the rationalist and universalist outlook of the Age of Enlightenment. He thought that people everywhere wanted, and deserved, much the same thing. (p. 428)

Voltaire and the philosophes had expected all peoples to progress along the same path of reason and enlightenment toward the same civilization. Herder and other thinkers thought that all peoples should develop their own genius in their own way. (p. 437)

Romanticism, unlike the Enlightenment, stressed the differences rather than the similarities of mankind. (p. 437)

The peacemakers at the Congress of Vienna hoped that a proper balance of power would also produce a lasting peace. (p. 446)

The Holy Alliance, probably sincerely meant by Alexander as a condemnation of violence, was at first not taken seriously by those who signed it and who thought it absurd to mix Christianity with politics. (p. 451)

The peacemakers were hostile both to democracy and to nationalism, the potent forces of the coming age. (p. 451)

XI.
REACTION VERSUS PROGRESS, 1815–1848
SECTIONS 52–57, pp. 453–499

52. *The Industrial Revolution in Britain*

Study Questions

1. What is meant by the Industrial Revolution? Why may it be said that it was not a "revolution" at all?
2. Of what basic significance for the Industrial Revolution in Great Britain was the Agricultural Revolution? Why and how was the older system of cultivation superseded?
3. What combination of circumstances helped to create a favorable environment for the emergence of machine industry in Britain?
4. Describe the changes that took place in Britain from about 1780 to 1840 (a) in the textile industry and (b) in other industries. What can one learn from the chart on p. 462 about the shift in sources of income in Britain during those years?
5. What important population and urban changes accompanied the Industrial Revolution in Britain? Why was it difficult to deal with the problems of rapid urbanization? (See also map, p. 460.)
6. How did the new factory system affect the working classes?
7. Explain the attitude toward government regulation of business of (a) the new "cotton lords," (b) the classical economists.

Key Discussion Sentences

In the years 1780 to 1815 political revolution, mainly on the Continent, and economic revolution, mostly in England, went on to a surprising degree independently of each other.

Without the transformation of farming by the English landowners, the Industrial Revolution probably could not have occurred.

Only a country like England, already wealthy from commerce and agriculture, could have been the first to initiate the machine age.

For working people in England, the Industrial Revolution was a hard experience, but earlier conditions had been difficult also.

Political economy as taught in grim Manchester was not without reason called the "dismal science."

Identifications

"squirearchy"	George Stephenson	Ricardo's "iron law of
enclosure acts	power loom	wages"
John Kay	Factory Act of 1802	laissez faire
Richard Arkwright	Adam Smith	free trade
James Watt	Malthus	
spinning jenny		

53. *The Advent of the "Isms"*

Study Questions

1. How may an "ism" be defined? Which "isms" still important today made their appearance in the years immediately after 1815? Why did they first emerge in those years?
2. How did the attitudes of romanticism differ from those of the Enlightenment?
3. What beliefs in political and economic matters did nineteenth-century liberals generally share?
4. What position did the English Radicals take toward the political and social conditions of their day? the republicans on the Continent? the early socialists?
5. Why was nationalism inherently revolutionary in this age? Comment on the preoccupation with nationalism in the early nineteenth century (a) in Germany, (b) in eastern Europe.

Key Discussion Sentences

After 1815 the combined forces of industrialization and of the French Revolution led to the multiplication of doctrines and movements of many sorts.

Nineteenth-century liberals believed above all in rational self-government.

The early socialists all regarded the existing economic system of private enterprise as aimless, chaotic, and outrageously unjust; they favored some degree of common ownership of productive assets.

The nationalists began with cultural nationalism and moved on to political nationalism.

Deeper than other "isms" was the profound current of humanitarianism in the nineteenth century.

After 1815 liberalism, radicalism, republicanism, socialism, and nationalism were the political forces driving Europe toward a future still unknown.

Identifications

Gothic Revival	Joseph Mazzini	Slavic Revival
Liberal	*Grimm's Fairy Tales*	*History of the Czech*
liberalism	Hegelian dialectic	*People*
Philosophical Radicals	Leopold von Ranke	Slavophilism
Jeremy Bentham	Friedrich List	Edmund Burke
Robert Owen	Charles Fourier	Carbonari
Count de Saint-Simon	Louis Blanc	

54. The Dike and the Flood: Domestic

Study Questions

1. Explain the principal objectives after 1815 of the governments that had defeated Napoleon. Why was it difficult to maintain political stability?
2. What political developments were taking place in France under Louis XVIII and his successor?
3. Why did the regime established for Poland by the Vienna peace settlement fail to work?
4. Describe nationalist activities in the German states in the years after 1815. What action did Metternich take?
5. Describe the cycle of popular unrest and government repression in Great Britain after 1815. How did economic factors contribute to the spread of political radicalism?
6. How would you summarize the domestic policies followed in almost every European country immediately after 1815?
7. What is meant by the "dike" and the "flood" in the title of this section? How does it apply in the case of (a) France, (b) Poland, (c) the German states, (d) Great Britain?

Key Discussion Sentences

In the years after 1815, the forces of the political right denounced all signs of liberalism as dangerous concessions to revolution.

National ideas in Germany carried with them a kind of liberal-democratic opposition to aristocrats, princes, and kings.

The reaction after 1815 was due only in part to memories of the French Revolution. It was due even more to the fear of revolution in the present.

Identifications

Metternich
Alexander I
Duke de Berry
Charles X
"white terror"
"more royalist than the
  king"

"Congress Poland"
Burschenschaft
Wartburg congress
Carlsbad Decrees
Corn Laws

"Peterloo massacre"
Six Acts
"Cato Street
  Conspiracy"

55. The Dike and the Flood: International

Study Questions

1. Explain the origin of the congresses of the Great Powers held in the years after 1815. What was their long-range significance?
2. What did the Congress of Aix-la-Chapelle decide with respect to France? What happened to Alexander's proposals for international action?
3. What events led to the summoning of the Congress of Troppau? Why could Metternich win Alexander to his views yet fail to persuade Castlereagh and the British? How was the revolution in Naples handled?
4. Describe the events that led to the Congress of Verona. What happened to the Greek effort at revolution? How was the revolution in Spain handled? With what results?
5. Explain the background and nature of the movement for independence in Latin America. What position did the British take? the United States? What were the results by about 1825?
6. Explain the nature and results of the revolt in Russia after Alexander's death.
7. Why did the congresses after 1815 fail to make progress toward an international order? With what consequences for liberalism in Europe?

Key Discussion Sentences

The British would assume no obligation to act upon indefinite and unforeseeable future events.

Over three hundred years of European colonial empires in the Americas came to an end, with a few exceptions, in the half-century following the independence of the United States.

The Monroe Doctrine may be thought of as a counterblast to Metternich.

Ten years after the defeat of Napoleon, the new forces issuing from the French Revolution seemed to be checked.

Identifications

Holy Alliance	Ypsilanti's "Greek"	Simón Bolívar
"congress system"	project	José de San Martín
protocol of Troppau	"creoles"	Joseph Bonaparte
	"peninsulars"	Monroe Doctrine
		Decembrist revolt

Map Exercise

1. On the basis of the discussion in the text, p. 482, and the map "The World about 1970," pp. 980–981, explain the statement: "It was only later in the nineteenth century that the map of South and Central America took form as we know it today."

56. The Breakthrough of Liberalism in the West: Revolutions of 1830–1832

Study Questions

1. Explain the nature and outcome of the Greek independence movement. What other results emerged from the Near Eastern crisis of the late 1820s?
2. What accounted for the July Revolution in France? Explain the division of opinion in the groups that had favored the revolution. How was the conflict resolved?
3. Discuss the constitutional and political changes that took place under Louis Philippe's regime. Which classes were the beneficiaries? Which groups remained dissatisfied?
4. What immediate effects did the Revolution of 1830 in France have throughout Europe? What arrangements made by the Congress of Vienna were now undone?
5. Explain the effect upon England of the Revolution of 1830 in France. Describe the events that led to the passage of the Reform Bill of 1832 and the major accomplishments of the act. How close to revolution was Britain?
6. Summarize the reforms introduced in Britain after 1832. Of what significance for the British economy was the repeal of the Corn Laws?

Key Discussion Sentences

The dike of reaction broke in 1830, and from that time on the stream of liberalism could not be stopped in western Europe.

To the beneficiaries of the Revolution of 1830, the July monarchy was the consummation and stopping place of political progress.

Never in the five hundred years of its history had the House of Commons been so unrepresentative as in the years before the Reform Bill of 1832.

The Reform Bill of 1832 was in its way a revolution.

After 1846 free trade would long be the rule for Britain.

Identifications

July Ordinances
Louis Philippe
pays légal
Tory reforms of the
  1820s
Catholic Emancipation
  Act

Duke of Wellington
Municipal Corporations
  Act
Lord Ashley
Factory Act of 1833

Mines Act of 1842
Ten Hours Act of 1847
Anti-Corn Law League
Lord Palmerston

57. Triumph of the West-European Bourgeoisie

Study Questions

1. Why may the decades immediately following 1830 be thought of as a kind of golden age of the west-European bourgeoisie? How did the "stake in society" theory apply to France and Great Britain in these years?
2. Describe the major economic developments taking place in this age.
3. What attitudes were emerging among working people in France and in Britain? What avenues were open to them for the improvement of their position?
4. Describe the objectives, nature, and results of the Chartist movement. What change took place in British labor after the 1840s?
5. What general observations may be made about Europe in the years between 1815 and 1848? What do the paintings by Delacroix and Daumier (pp. 486 and 493) reveal about (a) mid-nineteenth-century conceptions of revolution and (b) the triumph of the bourgeoisie?

Key Discussion Sentences

The reigning liberal doctrine of the years 1830–1848 was the theory that those should govern who have something to lose.

The dominant economic doctrine emphasized the conception of a free labor market.

The bourgeoisie, formerly identified in contrast to the nobility, was now identified in contrast to the working class.

In France socialism after 1830 blended with radical republicanism.

The bourgeois age had the effect of estranging the world of labor.

From 1815 to 1848, the forces set free by the French and Industrial Revolutions—liberalism, conservatism, nationalism, republicanism, democracy, and socialism—were all at work, and no stabilization had yet been achieved.

Identifications

bourgeoisie	Manchester School	Chartism
July Monarchy	Poor Law of 1834	

GENERAL ESSAY QUESTIONS FOR CHAPTER XI

1. Why may the period 1815–1848 be summarized as years of struggle between "reaction" and "progress"? How did conservative forces in these years oppose liberal change (a) domestically, (b) in international affairs? What was the status of the struggle by 1830–1832? by 1848?
2. Analyze the doctrines and movements stimulated by industrialization and the French Revolution, and explain the continuing importance of each of these doctrines and movements in our own time.
3. How did the Industrial Revolution build upon and carry forward the commercial capitalism of the early modern centuries? What were the social consequences of the new industrialism for the working classes?
4. Discuss the growing division between western and eastern Europe during the years 1815–1848. By 1848 what major problems did each face?

GENERAL DISCUSSION PASSAGES FOR CHAPTER XI

It may be (the matter is arguable) that the Industrial Revolution was more important than the French Revolution or any other. (pp. 453–454)

In a telescopic view of world history the two biggest changes experienced by the human race in the past ten thousand years may have been the agricultural or Neolithic revolution which ushered in the first civilizations and the Industrial Revolution which has ushered in the civilization of the nineteenth and twentieth centuries. (p. 454)

Industrialism and capitalism are by no means the same. Industrial society arose in the nineteenth century within capitalism. In the twentieth century, since the Russian Revolution, industrial societies have been created in which capitalism is rejected. (p. 454)

By the twentieth century the Industrial Revolution provoked a retaliation, in which some countries tried to industrialize, desperately hoping to catch up with the West while loudly denouncing it as imperialistic and capitalistic. (p. 455)

The Industrial Revolution is still going on; in some countries industrialization is barely beginning, and even in the most highly developed countries it is still making advances. (p. 455)

The new industrialists wanted to be let alone. They considered it unnatural to interfere with business, and they believed that, if allowed to follow their own judgment, they would assure the prosperity and progress of the country. (p. 461)

For working people the Industrial Revolution was a hard experience, yet the concentration of workers in city and factory opened the way to improvement of their condition. Workers developed a sense of solidarity, class interest, and common political aims. (p. 463)

The romantics loved the moods and impressions that the intellect could not classify, insisted on the value of feeling as well as of reason, were aware of the importance of the subconscious, and believed in original and creative genius that made its own rules and laws. (pp. 464–465)

Conservatism held that every people must change its institutions by gradual adaptation, and that no people could suddenly realize in the present any freedoms not already well prepared for in the past. This doctrine lacked appeal for those to whom the past had been a series of misfortunes. (p. 473)

The humanitarianism of the age consisted in a heightened awareness of cruelty inflicted upon others. To degrade human beings, use them as work animals, torture them, confine them unjustly, hold them as hostages for others, tear apart their families, and punish their relatives were regarded as foreign to true civilization. (p. 474)

The congresses of the Great Powers after 1815 resembled, in a tentative and partial way, the League of Nations after the First World War and the United Nations after the Second. (p. 478)

The dissensions that long continued to afflict Latin America were all present within the independence movement itself. (p. 481)

Western Europe, from 1815 to 1848, was growing collectively richer, more liberal, more bourgeois. The West, however, had not solved its social problems; its whole material civilization rested upon a restless and sorely tried working class. (p. 499)

From 1815 to 1848 there was repression everywhere, in varying degree, and apprehension. But there was also hope, confidence in the progress of an industrial and scientific society, and faith in the unfinished program of the rights of man. (p. 499)

XII.
REVOLUTION AND THE REIMPOSITION OF ORDER, 1848–1870
SECTIONS 58–62, pp. 500–531
PICTURE ESSAY, pp. 533–541

58. Paris: The Specter of Social Revolution in the West

Study Questions

1. Why did revolutions break out in so many different places at once in Europe in 1848? What may be said in general about these revolutions?
2. What pressures in the July Monarchy led to the abdication of Louis Philippe?
3. Describe the composition and policies of the Provisional Government in France after the February Revolution. What division existed within it?
4. Discuss the background and significance of the June Days of 1848. How did contemporaries react?
5. How would you explain the election of Louis Napoleon Bonaparte as president in December 1848? Describe his subsequent political maneuvers. What were the results?

Key Discussion Sentences

The July Monarchy in France was a platform of boards built over a volcano.

Seven of the ten members of the Provisional Government were "political" republicans, to whom the main issue was the form of government rather than the form of society; three were "social" republicans.

The June Days sent a shudder throughout France and Europe.

For twenty years a groundswell had been stirring the popular mind. It was known as the Napoleonic Legend.

Louis Napoleon Bonaparte was supposed to be a friend of the common man and at the same time a believer in order.

By 1851, the Second Republic was dead, as were liberalism and constitutionalism.

Identifications

Louis Philippe
Guizot
Lamartine
Louis Blanc
Labor Commission
National Workshops

Constituent Assembly
General Cavaignac
Chartism
Second French
   Republic
Napoleonic Ideas

Extinction of Poverty
Legitimists
Orleanists
Falloux law
coup d'état of Decem-
   ber 2, 1851

59. Vienna: The Nationalist Revolution in Central Europe and Italy

Study Questions

1. Describe the nature of the Austrian Empire in 1848. What attitude did Metternich maintain toward nationalism and liberal reform in the empire?
2. What revolutionary developments took place in March 1848 in the Austrian Empire? in Prussia and the other German states? in Italy?
3. What factors account for the ebbing of the revolutionary tide after June 1848?
4. Describe the victories of the counterrevolution between June 1848 and December 1848. How did division in the ranks of the revolutionaries contribute to their defeat?
5. What new revolutionary developments occurred in the first half of 1849? Explain their outcome.
6. Discuss the changes in attitudes and policies that took place in central Europe and in Italy immediately following the Revolution of 1848.

Key Discussion Sentences

The Austrian Empire of the Habsburgs included about a dozen recognizably different nationalities or language groups, and its political authority also reached far beyond its borders.

In March 1848 everything in the Austrian system collapsed with incredible swiftness.

The revolutions of 1848 failed partly because of the strength of the old governments and partly because of weakness and disunity within the revolutionary groups.

With the failure of the nationalist upheaval of 1848 in central Europe and Italy, reaction or antirevolutionism became the order of the day.

Identifications

March Days
Louis Kossuth
March Laws

Prague Assembly
Kremsier constitution
Magyar

Mazzini
Roman Republic
Pius IX

Frankfurt Assembly	Jellachich	*Syllabus of Errors*
Charles Albert	Windischgrätz	Prince Schwarzenberg
Ferdinand I	Francis Joseph	Bach system

Map Exercises

1. Study the map of Europe in 1815 on pp. 448–449 and the maps on pp. 222 and 470. (a) What were the boundaries of the Austrian Empire in 1848? Name the principal subdivisions of the empire. In what other areas of Europe was Austrian political influence dominant? (b) Which nationalities and language groups were within the Austrian Empire in 1848? How were they distributed? (c) Examining the map of Europe in 1923 on pp. 728–729, explain which countries were part of the Habsburg empire in 1848.
2. Can you locate each of the places mentioned in Section 59?

60. Frankfurt and Berlin: The Question of a Liberal Germany

Study Questions

1. What seemed to be the major obstacle to German unification? other obstacles?
2. Describe Prussia in the years before 1848. Which aspects of Prussian development seemed illiberal? Which seemed forward-looking?
3. What position did Frederick William IV take when revolution broke out in Prussia? Explain the status of the revolution by the end of 1848.
4. How did the origin of the Frankfurt Assembly contribute both to its strength and to its weakness? Of what significance was its desire to retain non-German peoples?
5. Explain the decisions that the Frankfurt Assembly reached on the nature of the new Germany, and the outcome of the assembly's proposals.
6. Why did Frederick William IV's plan for a German union fail? What kind of constitution did Prussia itself receive in 1850?
7. What general observations may be made about the failure of the German unification movement of 1848?

Key Discussion Sentences

The Frankfurt Assembly was attempting to bring a unified German state into being which would also be liberal and constitutional.

The members of the Frankfurt Assembly, with a handful of exceptions, were not revolutionary.

The most troublesome question facing the Frankfurt Assembly was not social but national.

The Frankfurt Assembly became fatally dependent upon the Austrian and Prussian armies.

In 1848 liberal nationalism failed in Germany, and a less gentle kind of nationalism soon replaced it.

Identifications

Frederick William IV
Zollverein
Berlin Assembly
Great Germans *vs.*
  Little Germans

Declaration of the
  Rights of the German
  People
"Forty-eighters"

humiliation of Olmütz
Prussian constitution of
  1850

Map Exercises

1. Study the map of Europe in 1815 on pp. 448–449 and the map, "The German Question, 1815–1871" on p. 555. How did the delegates at the Frankfurt Assembly differ over the boundaries of the Germany they wished to unify? Explain the position taken by (a) the Great Germans and (b) the Little Germans. What proposal was finally agreed upon?
2. Can you locate each of the places mentioned in Section 60?

61. *The New Toughness of Mind: Realism, Positivism, Marxism*

Study Questions

1. What may be said about the accomplishments, failures, and indirect consequences of the Revolution of 1848?
2. Analyze the moral reorientation that took place after 1848. How was the new toughness of mind reflected in literature and the arts? in attitudes toward science? in religion? in basic philosophical thought? in new attitudes in domestic and international affairs?
3. How would you analyze the principal sources of Marxism? How did Marxism dramatize the existing conditions of the working classes?
4. How did Marx explain the nature of capitalist crises and depressions? Explain the nature and the significance for Marx of dialectical materialism. How did Marx's views differ from those of Hegel?
5. Summarize the picture of the past, present, and future offered by Marxism. What were the implications for the working class of the existing war between the bourgeoisie and the proletariat?
6. How would you explain the advantages and handicaps of Marxism in winning supporters?

Key Discussion Sentences

The dreams of half a century were all blasted in 1848. After that year a new toughness of mind could be detected everywhere.

Although Marxism began to be a historical force in the 1870s, it grew out of the 1840s and reflected the conditions of that period.

Marxism may be said to have merged French revolutionism, the British Industrial Revolution, and German philosophy.

One of the advantages of Marxism was its claim to be scientific.

Some elements of Marxism stood in the way of its natural propagation.

Identifications

"realism"
positivism
Auguste Comte
Realpolitik
Friedrich Engels
Communist Manifesto
Capital

*Condition of the Work-
    ing Classes in
    England*
"surplus value"
materialist conception
    of history
Young Hegelians

"dictatorship of the pro-
    letariat"
"withering away" of
    the state
"scientific socialism"
"utopian socialism"

62. *Bonapartism: The Second French Empire, 1852–1870*

PICTURE ESSAY: EARLY INDUSTRIALISM AND SOCIAL CLASSES
(pp. 533–541)

Study Questions

1. Discuss political institutions and political life in the Second Empire.
2. Describe French economic growth under Napoleon III. What gains did working people make in these years?
3. Explain Napoleon III's attitude toward free trade. Of what significance were the 1860s for the development of free trade in Europe?
4. What kind of opposition to Napoleon III developed? What caused the ruin and downfall of the Second Empire?
5. Why may Napoleon III be looked upon as a precursor of a later age?
6. How do the illustrations and accompanying text in the Picture Essay illustrate social and economic trends in England and France in the nineteenth century?

Key Discussion Sentences

There is no doubt that Napoleon III became dictator on a wave of popular acclaim.

Napoleon III claimed to bring together mass democracy, intelligent government, and economic prosperity.

Napoleon III held that forms of government were less important than economic or social realities.

It was as a social engineer that Napoleon III preferred to be known.

Identifications

Baron Haussmann	*Crédit Foncier*	free trade treaty of
Saint-Simonians	Suez Canal	1860
"socialist emperor"	law of "limited	Liberal Empire
Crédit Mobilier	liability"	

GENERAL ESSAY QUESTIONS FOR CHAPTER XII

1. What common objectives were sought by the revolutionists in Europe in 1848? To what extent were they successful? How did the outcome lead to a new "toughness of mind" and new strategies?
2. How were the ideas of Marxism derived from (a) the French Revolution, (b) social and economic conditions of the time, and (c) German philosophy? What relationship did Marxism have to earlier and later forms of socialism? to later communism?
3. In what sense may Louis Napoleon Bonaparte be considered the first "modern" dictator? Discuss (a) his coming to power, (b) his rule as Napoleon III.

GENERAL DISCUSSION PASSAGES FOR CHAPTER XII

The fundamental problem of the century, the bringing of peoples into some kind of mutual and moral relationship with their governments, was ignored by responsible authorities. (p. 509)

The tragedy of Germany (and hence of Europe) lay in the fact that the German Revolution of 1848 came too late—at a time when social revolutionaries had already begun to declare war on the bourgeoisie and the bourgeoisie was already afraid of the common man. (p. 516)

The failure to produce a democratic Germany was long one of the overshadowing facts of modern times. (p. 514)

It is the common man, not the professor or respectable merchant, who in unsettled times actually seizes firearms and rushes to shout revolutionary words in the streets. Without lower-class insurrection not even middle-class revolutions have been successful. (p. 516)

Realpolitik means that governments should not be guided by ideology, by any desire to defend or promote any particular view of the world, but should follow their own practical interests, meet facts and situations as they arise, make any alliances that seem useful, disregard tastes and scruples, and use any practical means to achieve their ends. (p. 521)

Many believed that the promise of the French Revolution had not yet been fulfilled, since social and economic equality had not followed the civil and legal equality already won. (p. 522)

Among other things the Communist Manifesto announced that the state was a committee of the bourgeoisie for the exploitation of the people, that religion was a drug to keep the worker quietly dreaming upon imaginary heavenly rewards, and that the proletariat had no country but only common interests and a common enemy. (p. 523)

According to Marx, the "relations of production" (technology, property systems, etc.) determine what kind of religions, philosophies, governments, laws, and moral values people accept. Law is the will of the stronger (i.e., the stronger class); "right" and "justice" are thin emanations of class interest. (pp. 525–526)

Marxism was a strong compound of the scientific, the historical, the metaphysical, and the apocalyptic. (p. 526)

Had the old Europe not gone to pieces in the twentieth-century wars, and had Marxism not been revived by Lenin and transplanted to Russia, it is probable that Marx's ideas would have been domesticated into the general body of European thought, and much less said about them in modern history. (p. 527)

Not until the 1920s and 1930s, when dictators sprouted all over Europe, did the world begin to suspect what Louis Napoleon Bonaparte had really been, an omen of the future rather than a bizarre reincarnation of the past. (p. 531)

XIII.
THE
CONSOLIDATION
OF LARGE NATION-
STATES, 1859–1871
SECTIONS 63–70, pp. 542–582

63. Backgrounds: The Idea of the Nation-State

Study Questions

1. What is the meaning of nationalism? the nation-state? Of what special importance for the growth of nationalism were the years after 1860?
2. Of what significance was the Crimean War for European national movements? How did the major European powers become involved in the dispute that broke out between Russia and Turkey in 1853?

Key Discussion Sentences

The idea of the nation-state has served both to bring people together into larger units and to break them apart into smaller ones.

The consolidation of large nation-states involved territorial unification as well as the creation of new ties between government and governed.

Many of the liberal and nationalist aims which the revolutionists of 1848 had failed to achieve were accomplished in the years 1859–1871, but only through a series of wars.

64. Cavour and the Italian War of 1859: The Unification of Italy

Study Questions

1. Describe the state of political affairs in Italy in the 1850s. How did Piedmont differ from the other Italian states?
2. Explain the background and nature of the movement for national unification in Italy. What role had Mazzini played? What had happened in 1848 to the unification movement?

3. Explain the political, economic, and social views of Cavour. How did he differ from Mazzini in his program for Italian unification?
4. Describe the steps Cavour took to unite Italy. How successful was he? What events followed the French withdrawal from the war against Austria?
5. How did Cavour react to Garibaldi's successes? What was the status of unification in 1861? How was it eventually completed?

Key Discussion Sentences

In Italy there was a widespread desire for a liberal national state in which all Italy might be included.

Cavour shared in the new toughness of mind that prevailed after 1848.

Italy was united by the long high-minded apostolate of Mazzini, the audacity of Garibaldi, the cold policy of Cavour, war and insurrection, and armed violence endorsed by popular vote.

Persistent problems troubled Italy after unification.

Identifications

Risorgimento	Orsini	War of 1859
Victor Emmanuel	"Garibaldi's Thousand"	Magenta
Savoy	Crimean War	Solferino
Piedmont	Napoleon III	*Italia irredenta*
Sardinia		

Map Exercise

1. On the outline map of Europe, top panel, (a) show the separate political divisions of Italy in 1815, (b) indicate the year in which each of these states became part of united Italy. Suggested source: *A History of the Modern World,* pp. 546–551, and map, p. 549.

65. *Bismarck: The Founding of a German Empire*

Study Questions

1. What lessons for national unification did the failure of the Frankfurt Assembly seem to teach? How did economic and social changes affect German nationalist attitudes?
2. Explain Bismarck's political outlook and describe the nature and outcome of his dispute with the liberals in the Prussian parliament. What was the meaning of his famous "blood and iron" statement?
3. How did Bismarck succeed in ousting Austria from a position of leadership in Germany?

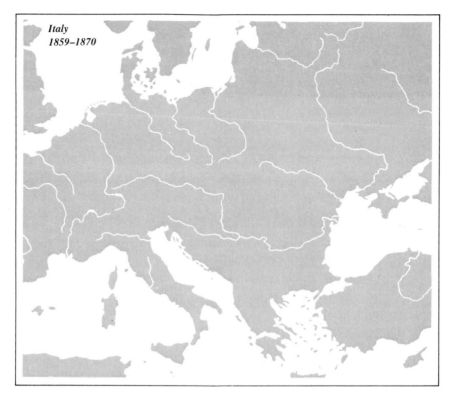

Italy
1859–1870

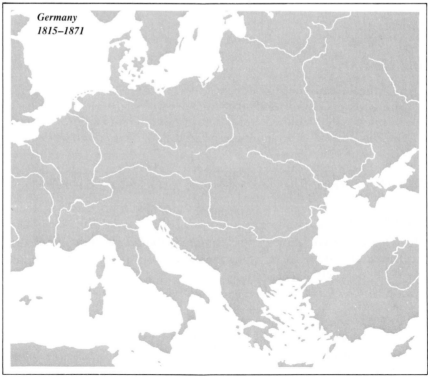

Germany
1815–1871

Unification of Italy and Germany

4. Describe the membership, structure, and constitution of the North German Confederation. What use did Bismarck make of existing democratic sentiment? socialist sentiment?
5. What did Bismarck hope to accomplish by a war with France? Describe the background of the Franco-Prussian War. How did the war affect France? Germany?
6. Which provisions of the new German constitution were democratic? Which provisions were neither liberal nor democratic?

Key Discussion Sentences

Bismarck was not a German nationalist but a Prussian.

Bismarck became the classic practitioner of *Realpolitik*.

German unification was accomplished in three short wars.

The Germans did not unify themselves by their own exertions; the German Empire that emerged from the nationalist movement was a Germany conquered by Prussia.

The new German constitution guaranteed the preponderant influence of Prussia in the German Empire.

Identifications

German confederation
  of 1815
Junker
Schleswig-Holstein
  question
Danish War
Seven Weeks' War

battle of Sadowa
North German
  Confederation
Ferdinand Lassalle
"Ems dispatch"
battle of Sedan

siege of Paris
treaty of Frankfurt
"indemnity act" of
  1867
Prussian constitution of
  1850

Map Exercises

1. On the outline map of Europe, bottom panel, (a) show the boundaries of the German Empire in 1871, (b) indicate the dates by which the major states became part of the empire, (c) shade the area forming the Kingdom of Prussia in 1871. Suggested source: *A History of the Modern World*, pp. 230–231, 555, and 562–563.
2. Compare the map of Europe in 1815 (pp. 448–449), in 1871 (pp. 562–563), in 1923 (pp. 728–729), and in the contemporary period (front end papers). Explain this statement: "The map of Europe from 1871 to 1918 was the simplest it has ever been before or since." (p. 543)

66. The Dual Monarchy of Austria-Hungary

Study Questions

1. What were the chief problems confronting the Habsburg empire in the nineteenth century? What did its recent wars demonstrate about the empire? Explain the special attitudes of the Magyars.
2. How would you evaluate the Compromise of 1867 as a solution to the nationalities problem in the Habsburg empire? Which groups were the real beneficiaries?
3. Discuss political changes in both Austria and Hungary after 1867. What may be said about the economic and social structure of the Dual Monarchy?

Key Discussion Sentences

The essential question, in a nationalist age, was how the Habsburg government would react to the problems raised by the insistence on national rights.

The Compromise of 1867 was essentially a bargain between the Germans of Austria-Bohemia and the Magyars of Hungary.

Identifications

Austroslavism	Dual Monarchy	Count Beust
Francis Joseph	*Ausgleich*	

67. Liberalization in Tsarist Russia: Alexander II

Study Questions

1. How did the autocracy in Russia differ from absolutism in the West?
2. Explain the role of the "intelligentsia" in Russian life.
3. How did serfdom in Russia before 1861 differ from and resemble American slavery? What did the Act of Emancipation of 1861 accomplish?
4. Summarize the legal and judicial reforms introduced by Alexander II and the steps taken in the direction of self-government.
5. How did the Russian revolutionists react to the reforms of Alexander II? Indicate the additional steps taken by Alexander in 1880 to win liberal support. What changes took place under his successor?

Key Discussion Sentences

Tsarist Russia shared in the liberal movement of the late nineteenth century.

Even after emancipation, the peasants did not possess their land according to principles of private property, nor did they possess full individual freedom of action.

Identifications

Alexander II	"Third Section"	Alexander Herzen
Westernizers	*mir*	Bakunin
Slavophiles	Act of Emancipation	People's Will
muzhik	redemption money	Alexander III
	zemstvos	
	nihilists	

68. The United States: The American Civil War

Study Questions

1. Describe the growth of population in the United States during the nineteenth century. How were the problems created by immigration being met?
2. How did the Industrial Revolution affect the growing estrangement of North and South? How did the westward movement intensify the slavery quarrel?
3. Explain the immediate background to the American Civil War and the nature of the struggle. What attitudes did Europeans take toward the war?
4. What conception of the United States prevailed after the victory of the North? What may be considered the most far-reaching result of the American Civil War?
5. How was slavery abolished? What may be said about the sweeping nature of this step?
6. What did the Reconstruction period after the Civil War accomplish and fail to accomplish?
7. Discuss economic changes during the Civil War and in the period immediately following.

Key Discussion Sentences

By 1860 a sense of sectionalism had developed in the South, not different in principle from the nationalism felt by many peoples in Europe.

With the Civil War, the idea triumphed that the United States was a national state, composed not of member states but of a unitary people irrevocably bound together.

The Reconstruction period may be compared to the most advanced phase of the French Revolution.

In the 1870s the Southern whites gradually regained control by what Europeans would call a counterrevolution.

After the Civil War, industry and finance dominated national politics in the increasingly centralized United States.

Identifications

Mexican War	Thirteenth Amendment	Morrill tariff
"Missouri	Fourteenth Amendment	Union Pacific Railroad
Compromise"	Reconstruction	Homestead Act
"Compromise of 1850"	"radical republicans"	
abolitionists		
Emancipation		
Proclamation		

69. The Dominion of Canada, 1867

Study Questions

1. What sources of friction were there in Canada in the early part of the nineteenth century?
2. Summarize (a) the significant provisions of the Earl of Durham's Report of 1839 and (b) the action taken as a consequence of the report.
3. What did the British North America Act of 1867 provide? Why was a federal plan rejected? What further developments took place in the years after 1867?
4. What was the long-range significance of the "dominion" idea?

Key Discussion Sentences

After 1867 the Dominion of Canada moved from control over internal affairs to control over external matters.

Canada pioneered in the development of the "dominion" idea.

Identifications

Quebec Act of 1774	Lower Canada	"responsible
United Empire	Upper Canada	government"
Loyalists	rebellion of 1837	"dominion status"

Map Exercise

1. Study the map on p. 549, "Nation Building, 1859–1867." What similar developments were taking place in the four areas shown? What parallel developments were taking place in Germany? (See map, p. 555.)

70. *Japan and the West*

Study Questions

1. What major developments were taking place in Japan during the years of seclusion from approximately 1640 to 1854? What parallels may be observed between the history of Japan and that of Europe? Why did the early Tokugawa shoguns exclude foreigners?
2. What is meant by the "opening" of Japan to the West? What potential allies did Perry find in 1853? Explain the nature of the commercial treaties signed.
3. What conclusion about dealing with the West did the anti-Westerners reach after 1854? How did they proceed?
4. Describe the westernization of Japan in the Meiji era (1868–1912). To what extent was the new parliamentary system faithful to liberal principles?
5. What general comments may be made about the westernization of Japan? What aspects of Western civilization did the Japanese seem most interested in adopting?

Key Discussion Sentences

When Japan was opened to the West by Commodore Perry in 1853, the Japanese were a highly civilized people living in a complex society.

In order to protect their own internal culture, the Japanese took over the external apparatus of Western civilization.

In opening Japan, the Europeans opened up more than they had anticipated.

Identifications

hereditary Tokugawa shogunate	Yedo	lords of Choshu and Satsuma
daimyo	Shinto	Emperor Mutsuhito
samurai	Commodore Perry	constitution of 1889
	extraterritoriality	

GENERAL ESSAY QUESTIONS FOR CHAPTER XIII

1. Nationalism has been one of the great driving forces in modern history. How may it be defined? What contributions to national ideas and movements were made by (a) the French Revolutionary and Napoleonic era, (b) the years 1815–1848, (c) the revolutions of 1848, (d) the years 1859–1871? Of what continuing importance has nationalism been in the twentieth century?
2. Compare and contrast the movements for national unification in Italy and Germany in the years 1815–1871, and their results. Of what special importance was political leadership in each case? How did *Realpolitik* apply in each instance?

3. What similar developments in national consolidation and nation-building may be observed over the years 1859–1871 in (a) Italy, (b) Germany, (c) Austria-Hungary, (d) Russia, (e) the United States, (f) Canada, (g) Japan?

GENERAL DISCUSSION PASSAGES FOR CHAPTER XIII

Since 1860 or 1870 a nation-state system has prevailed. The consolidation of nations in the nineteenth century became a model in the twentieth for other peoples, large and small. (p. 543)

For many in the nineteenth century, nationalism, the winning of national unity and independence and the creation of the nation-state, became a kind of secular faith. (p. 543)

A nation-state may be thought of as one in which supreme political authority somehow rests upon and represents the will and feeling of its inhabitants. There must be a people, not merely a swarm of human beings. Nations take form in many ways, but all are alike in feeling themselves to be communities, permanent communities in which individual persons, together with their children and their children's children, are committed to a collective destiny on earth. (pp. 543–544)

History, in the thought of Hegel, and after him Marx, became a vast force almost independent of human beings. History was said to ordain, require, necessitate, condemn, justify, or excuse. What one did not like could be dismissed as a mere historical phase. What one wanted could be described as historically necessary and bound to come. (p. 551)

In nineteenth-century Russia the intelligentsia sensed themselves as a class apart. They were made up of students, university graduates, and persons who had a good deal of leisure to read. They tended to sweeping and all-embracing philosophies. They believed that intellectuals should play a large role in society and formed an exaggerated idea of the direct influence of thinkers upon the course of historical change. (p. 566)

The westernization of Japan still stands as the most remarkable transformation ever undergone by any people in so short a time. (p. 582)

The apparatus of Western civilization—science, technology, machinery, arms, political and legal organization—was the part of Western civilization for which other peoples generally felt a need, and which they hoped to adopt without losing their own spiritual independence. Although these aspects of Western civilization were sometimes rather scornfully dismissed as materialistic, they became the common ground for the interdependent worldwide civilization that emerged at the close of the nineteenth century. (p. 582)

XIV.
EUROPEAN
CIVILIZATION,
1871–1914
SECTIONS 71–77, pp. 583–641

71. The "Civilized World"

Study Questions

1. Describe the materialistic achievements and nonmaterialistic values that led Europeans to think of themselves as the "civilized world."
2. What is meant by the inner and outer zones of Europe? Which areas outside Europe belonged to each? What third zone lay beyond the European world?
3. How do the paintings by Sheeler (p. 597) and by Seurat (p. 610) contribute to an understanding of late nineteenth-century European civilization?

Key Discussion Sentences

In the half-century from 1871 to 1914, Europe in many ways reached the climax of the modern phase of its civilization and also exerted its maximum influence upon peoples outside Europe.

The unity of Europe lay in the fact that Europeans (including inhabitants of countries that were European offshoots) shared a similar way of life and outlook.

Although the ideals of European civilization were in part materialistic, they were by no means exclusively so.

There were really two Europes.

Map Exercise

1. On the outline map of Europe, draw the boundary lines dividing the inner and outer zones of Europe (as they are described in the text) in the years 1871–1914. Suggested source: *A History of the Modern World*, pp. 586–587, and map, pp. 562–563.

72. Basic Demography: The Increase of the Europeans

Study Questions

1. Describe the major trends in world population growth since 1650 (a) in Europe and (b) in the world as a whole. What conclusions may be drawn from the table on p. 588? from the table on p. 1039?
2. Why did European birth rates begin to fall about 1880? In what sense was France a pioneer in that respect? What is meant by the "European family pattern"?
3. How do you explain the fact that despite rapid European population growth there was no serious problem of overpopulation as there is in many parts of the world today?
4. Describe the growth of city life between 1850 and 1914. What conclusions may be drawn from the statistical information in Appendix III of the text? What have been the effects of urban life upon the character of modern society?
5. What can be said about the nature and causes of the migration from Europe that took place in the century after 1840? What conclusions may be drawn from the map on p. 592 and the tables on pp. 593 and 594?

Key Discussion Sentences

All continents except Africa grew enormously in population in the three centuries following 1650, but it was Europe that grew the most.

The increase in population since 1650 can be attributed to falling death rates rather than to increasing birth rates.

The growth of cities between 1850 and 1914 was phenomenal.

The Atlantic Migration towers above all other historical migrations in magnitude, and possibly also in significance.

The exodus from Europe was due to a remarkable and temporary combination of causes. Perhaps the most basic was the underlying liberalism of the age.

73. The World Economy of the Nineteenth Century

Study Questions

1. What technological advances contributed to the "new Industrial Revolution" after 1870? How did these changes affect the major European countries? the United States?
2. What may be said about the status of free trade in the years 1846 to 1914? Explain the relationship between imports and exports (a) in the British economy and (b) in the economy of industrial Europe as a whole.

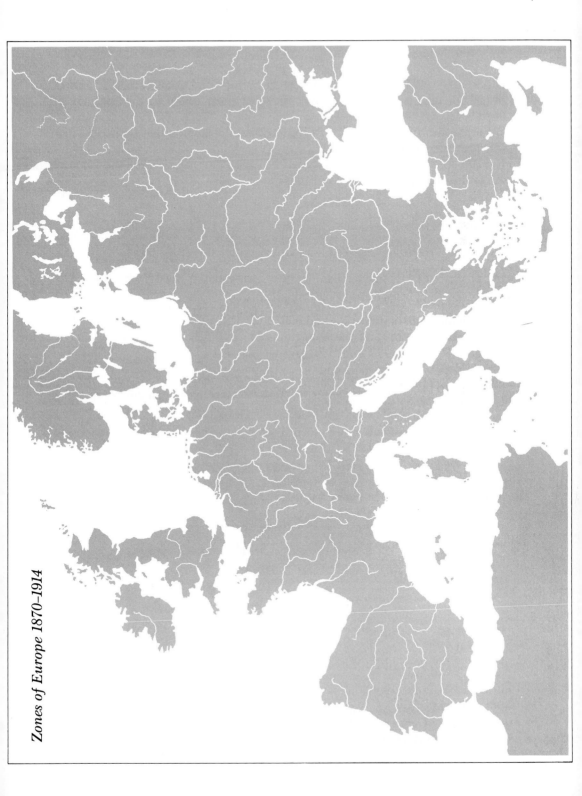

Zones of Europe 1870–1914

3. Of what significance was the export of capital from Europe? What role did each of the major European countries play? (See chart, p. 601.)
4. How did the gold standard facilitate international trade in this age? Describe London's special financial role.
5. Discuss the relationship between western Europe and other parts of the earth in the nineteenth-century economy. In what sense had a true world market been created?
6. What kinds of insecurity resulted from the capitalist economy? What devices were resorted to in order to combat insecurity?
7. Explain the important changes in capitalism about 1880. What were some of the political and social effects of these changes?

Key Discussion Sentences

The Industrial Revolution entered a new phase after the 1870s.

Britain, the pioneer in mechanization, was being outstripped in both the Old World and the New, in the years 1870 to 1914.

The great economic triumphs of the nineteenth century were the creation of an integrated world market and the financing and building up of countries outside Europe.

The nineteenth-century system of unregulated capitalism was extremely precarious, and the position of most people in this system was exceedingly vulnerable.

Identifications

"new Industrial Revolution"	invisible exports	"vertical" integration
balance of payments	the corporation	"horizontal" integration
	trusts and cartels	

74. *The Advance of Democracy: Third French Republic, United Kingdom, German Empire*

Study Questions

1. Of what significance was the Paris Commune in the formation of the Third French Republic?
2. Describe the machinery of government set up by the laws of 1875 in France. How was the role of the executive further clarified?
3. With what major problems was the Third Republic occupied in the years 1871 to 1914? How successfully did it cope with them?
4. What kind of government did Great Britain exemplify in the half-century before 1914? Explain the steps by which the suffrage was extended in the

years 1832 to 1918. Of what significance were the reforms of the Liberal government after 1906?

5. How successfully had Britain dealt with the Irish problem by 1914?
6. What general observations may be made about the political nature of the German Empire? Discuss the nature and results of Bismarck's conflict with (a) the Catholic church and (b) the Social Democrats. What was the motive behind his social insurance program?
7. In what direction did Germany seem to be moving under William II in the years before 1914?
8. Summarize briefly the major political developments in Italy, Austria-Hungary, and other European countries from 1871 to 1914. What general conclusions may be reached about the advance of political democracy?

Key Discussion Sentences

In the years 1871 to 1914, democratization often took place within a continuing monarchical and aristocratic framework.

Questions that in other countries were only party questions became questions of "regime" in France.

The political energies of the French republican statesmen went into liquidating the past.

The rise of labor in Britain and the Liberal reforms after 1906 had a deep impact upon the Liberal party and indeed upon liberalism itself.

The German Empire developed neither the strong constitutionalism of England nor the democratic equality of France, but by 1914 democratic forces were growing stronger.

Identifications

Marshal MacMahon	Reform Bills of 1867	Osborne Judgment
General Boulanger	and 1884	*Kulturkampf*
Dreyfus affair	Irish home rule	antisocialist laws
laic laws of 1905	David Lloyd George	William II
Radical Socialists	Parliament Act of 1911	Giolitti
Victorian era		

75. The Advance of Democracy: Socialism and Labor Unions

Study Questions

1. How did trade unionism in Britain differ from trade unionism on the Continent?
2. How did the British Labour party differ from socialist parties on the Continent?

3. Describe the origins and history of (a) the First International and (b) the Second International.
4. What political and economic developments contributed to the growth of revisionism in the socialist movement? Discuss the ideas and movements that arose in response.
5. What reasons are suggested for the decline in the revolutionary mood of the working class by 1914?

Key Discussion Sentences

Socialism and trade unionism were in some ways contradictory.

After 1880 Marxism turned into a less revolutionary "parliamentary socialism."

For the Fabians, socialism was the social and economic counterpart to political democracy, as well as its inevitable outcome.

The tendency to revisionism drove the really revolutionary spirits either to revolutionary syndicalism or to a reemphasis of orthodox Marxist fundamentals.

Identifications

"new model" unionism
industrial unions
British Labour party
Taff Vale decision
Bakunin
German Social Democratic party

Jules Guesde
Jean Jaurès
Fabian Society
Eduard Bernstein
revolutionary syndicalism

Georges Sorel
Karl Kautsky
Alexandre Millerand
Lenin
Bolsheviks

76. Science, Philosophy, the Arts, and Religion

Study Questions

1. Why was faith in science so widespread in the half-century before 1914?
2. Explain Charles Darwin's conclusions and analyze the impact of Darwinian evolution upon the general thought of the age. What is meant by Social Darwinism?
3. How did anthropology affect (a) race consciousness, (b) attitudes toward culture and morals, (c) religion?
4. How did Freud influence our understanding of human behavior? What contribution did Pavlov make?
5. How did discoveries in physics upset older views of matter and energy and other scientific concepts? What was Einstein's special contribution?
6. In what sense do the paintings by Monet (p. 584), Seurat (p. 610), Kandinsky (p. 632), Braque (p. 615), and others in later chapters in the text represent

the artistic revolution associated with modern art? What problems of communication between artist and public did these innovations raise?

7. How was the conflict between modernists and fundamentalists resolved in (a) Protestantism, (b) Roman Catholicism, (c) Judaism? What other trends and developments were observable in these religions?

Key Discussion Sentences

There never was a time when faith in the powers of natural science was so widespread as in the half-century preceding the First World War.

By about 1914 conceptions of the universe accepted since the time of Newton in the eighteenth century were being challenged on all sides.

The greatest impact upon the general thinking of the latter part of the nineteenth century came from biology and, in particular, from Darwin's theory of evolution.

The study by anthropologists of all kinds of cultures and societies tended to produce a relativism or skepticism about the values of one's own society.

Psychology, especially the work of Freud, led to thoroughly upsetting implications about the nature of human behavior.

Never had artist and society been so far apart.

Religion was more threatened after 1860 or 1870 than ever before.

Identifications

Origin of Species	agnosticism	Pius IX
T. H. Huxley	Herbert Spencer	*Syllabus of Errors*
Gregor Mendel	Friedrich Nietzsche	Vatican Council of 1870
Sir James Frazer	"higher" criticism of	Leo XIII
Sigmund Freud	the Bible	*Rerum Novarum*
Ivan Pavlov	David Friedrich Strauss	Lateran treaty of 1929
$e = mc^2$	Ernest Renan	Theodor Herzl

77. The Waning of Classical Liberalism

Study Questions

1. Explain the meaning of classical liberalism. What did it mean in political matters? in economic matters?

2. After 1880 what signs could be observed of the decline of economic liberalism within each industrial country?

3. What is meant by the new liberalism? How did it differ from classical liberalism and how resemble it?

4. How did nineteenth- and twentieth-century developments in biology and

psychology affect the older view of human beings as rational animals? What were the implications of these views?

5. What may be said of the late nineteenth-century philosophies glorifying struggle? How were they strengthened by actual historical events?
6. How did political and economic developments in England between 1900 and 1914 reflect the decline of classical liberalism?
7. How would you assess the strength of liberalism in Europe in 1914?

Key Discussion Sentences

The "new" liberalism rejected the principle of laissez faire.

Paradoxically, this great age of science found that human beings were not rational animals.

The end of the nineteenth century abounded in philosophies glorifying struggle and in writings embracing a frank rejection of reason.

The persistence and changing nature of liberalism, rather than its wane, should be emphasized at the conclusion of a chapter on European civilization in the half-century before 1914.

Identifications

economic liberalism	"realism"	*Reflections on Violence*
neomercantilism	"irrationalism"	suffragettes

GENERAL ESSAY QUESTIONS FOR CHAPTER XIV

1. Why may it be said that in the years 1871–1914 Europe reached the climax of the modern phase of its civilization? What major political, economic, and intellectual trends deserve to be stressed for these years?
2. Discuss (a) the continuing triumphs of liberalism and (b) the transformation and decline of liberalism in this age.
3. How did the growing self-consciousness of European labor manifest itself in the years 1871–1914?
4. How would you compare major developments in science, philosophy, the arts, and religion in the years 1871–1914 with those of the seventeenth and eighteenth centuries? with those of our own age?

GENERAL DISCUSSION PASSAGES FOR CHAPTER XIV

The ideals of European and Western civilization were profoundly moral, derived from Christianity but now secularized and detached from religion. (p. 584)

The essence of civilized life doubtless is in the intangibles, in the way in which people use their minds and in the attitudes they form toward others or toward the conduct and planning of their own lives. The intangibles, however, are not always agreed upon by persons of different cultures or ideologies. On the quantitative criteria there is less disagreement; all people, with few exceptions, wish to lower the death rate, raise the literacy rate, and increase human productivity. (p. 586)

The small family system, together with the decline of infant mortality, since they combined to free women from the interminable bearing and tending of infants, probably did more than anything else to improve the position of women. (p. 590)

The great city set the tone of modern society. (p. 591)

A new kind of private power had arisen, which its critics liked to call "feudal." Since no economic system had ever been so centralized up to that time, never in fact had so few people exercised so much economic power over so many. (p. 605)

Religion was more threatened than ever in the past, because never before had science or philosophies drawing upon science addressed themselves so directly to the existence of life and of man. Never before had so many of the fundamental premises of traditional religion been questioned or denied. (p. 631)

On the integration of the Jews into the larger community, the traditions of the Enlightenment and the liberalism of the nineteenth century agreed. But anti-Semitism was a barrier to assimilation, as in a different way was Zionism. (p. 637)

Freud's ideas, by revealing the wide areas of human behavior outside conscious control, suggested that human beings were not essentially rational creatures at all. (p. 628)

The arts followed the intellectual development of the age, reflecting, as they do today, relativism, irrationalism, social determinism, and interest in the subconscious. (p. 630)

Although classical liberalism was still thinking of adult males, the very principle of liberalism, with its stress on the autonomy of the individual, contributed to the still small but growing movement of women's rights. (p. 637)

The function of thought in some frankly irrationalist philosophy was to keep people agitated and excited and ready for action, not to achieve any correspondence with rational or objective truth. Sorel declared that violence was good irrespective of the end accomplished (so much did he hate existing society). Such ideas passed into fascism and other activist movements of the twentieth century. (p. 640)

XV.
EUROPE'S WORLD SUPREMACY
SECTIONS 78–84, pp. 642–682
PICTURE ESSAY, pp. 683–693

78. *Imperialism: Its Nature and Causes*

Study Questions

1. How may imperialism be defined? What major phases have there been in the history of European expansion?
2. How did the "new imperialism" differ from the colonialism of earlier times? What different gradations of European domination may be noted? How was European rule generally imposed?
3. Discuss the motives that lay behind European expansion in the late nineteenth century. Of what relative importance were economic pressures? the quest for security? nonpolitical and noneconomic motives?
4. With what "mission" was imperialism identified? How would you evaluate the attitude expressed in the lines by Kipling?

Key Discussion Sentences

In the short span of two decades, from about 1880 to 1900, the European countries partitioned the earth among themselves.

In the process of imperialist expansion, security, both political and economic, seemed to be an aim that was as important as wealth.

Imperialism became a crusade.

Identifications

colony	neomercantilism	*Imperialism, the Highest Stage of Capitalism*
protectorate	"surplus capital"	
sphere of influence	J. A. Hobson	
"sheltered markets"	Joseph Chamberlain	White Man's burden *mission civilisatrice*

79. *The Americas*

Study Questions

1. What policies toward Mexico did the United States follow in the years before 1870?
2. Explain and illustrate the attitudes and policies of the United States toward Latin America in the latter part of the nineteenth century.
3. Describe the origins of the Spanish-American War. What evidence was there of American imperialist interests in Cuba? What territorial acquisitions and other rights did the United States acquire as a result of the war?
4. Of what significance was President Theodore Roosevelt's policy in the case of Santo Domingo? What was the subsequent history of this policy?
5. How did the United States' annexation of the Hawaiian Islands illustrate American imperialism?
6. What were the general results of the relationship of the United States with Latin America in the age of imperialism?

Key Discussion Sentences

The Monroe Doctrine became an effective barrier to European territorial ambitions. On the other hand, south of the border the United States became the imperialist power feared above all others.

Every sign of the new imperialism showed itself unmistakably in American relations with Cuba.

The American acquisition of the Hawaiian Islands was as typical of the new imperialism as any episode in the history of any European empire.

Identifications

Monroe Doctrine	Venezuela boundary	"Theodore Roosevelt
Mexican War	dispute	Corollary" to the
Juárez	Panama revolution	Monroe Doctrine
Napoleon III's Mexico	sinking of the *Maine*	"dollar diplomacy"
plan	Platt Amendment	"good neighbor" policy
Maximilian		

80. *The Dissolution of the Ottoman Empire*

Study Questions

1. How did the Ottoman Empire differ from the European states in its political organization and nature? What efforts at reform were made from 1856 to 1876? How did the reform effort end?

2. Why was Turkey called the "sick man of Europe"? What losses of the empire could be noted by 1850? What territory did it still encompass?
3. Why were the British concerned about the Russo-Turkish War of 1877? How was a general war averted?
4. What problems persisted in the Ottoman Empire after 1878? Explain the major steps in the dissolution of the empire from 1908 to 1923.
5. How did Egypt become a British protectorate? How did the French react?
6. Of what significance for international relations was the rivalry for the spoils of the Ottoman Empire?

Key Discussion Sentences

The long decline of Turkey constituted the Eastern Question. The empire had survived largely because of the European balance of power.

The Crimean War stimulated Turkish efforts to reform and to westernize the state. For about twenty years following the reform edict of 1856, the Turks sought to accomplish these ends.

The Congress of Berlin of 1878 kept peace in Europe at the expense of Turkey.

The European balance of power both protected and dismembered Turkey at the same time.

Identifications

"capitulations"	Pan-Slavism	Berlin to Baghdad
Hatt-i Humayun	Suez Canal	railway
Abdul Aziz	treaty of San Stefano	Ismail
Midhat Pasha	"jingoism"	Colonel Arabi
Abdul Hamid	Congress of Berlin	Evelyn Baring
Young Turks		

Map Exercise

1. Study the map on p. 660, "The Dissolution of the Ottoman Empire." What successive stages may be observed in the territorial disintegration of the Ottoman Empire? What had happened to the empire by 1914? by 1923?

81. The Partition of Africa

Study Questions

1. Explain the process by which Africa was partitioned after 1870. How successful were attempts at international control in the partition of Africa?
2. Which areas were occupied and controlled by Germany, France, and Britain respectively? by other European powers?

3. How did the partition of Africa affect relations among the European powers?
4. How would you assess the impact of European control upon the African peoples?

Key Discussion Sentences

Missionaries, explorers, and individual adventurers first opened up the interior of Africa to Europe.

The Berlin conference of 1885 laid down certain rules of the game for expansion in Africa.

In the fifteen years from 1885 to 1900, the entire continent of Africa, with the exception of Ethiopia and Liberia, was parceled out.

Europeans all over Africa resorted to forced labor.

From 1885 to 1900 the Europeans in Africa came dangerously near to open blows.

Identifications

David Livingstone	Brussels conference of	Cecil Rhodes
H. M. Stanley	1889	Jameson Raid
Karl Peters	"indirect rule"	Boer War
Brazza	hut tax	Paul Kruger
Leopold II	Adowa	Union of South Africa
Berlin conference of	Fashoda crisis	
1885		
Congo Free State		

Map Exercises

1. Study the map on p. 665, "Precolonial Africa: Sites and Peoples." What do the map and caption tell you about developments in Africa before the penetration of the Europeans?
2. On the outline map of Africa show the recognized holdings of the European powers by 1914. Draw arrows indicating the direction of expansionist pressure of the Germans, the French, and the British about 1898. Suggested source: *A History of the Modern World*, p. 667.
3. Can you locate on the map each of the places mentioned in Section 81?
4. How has the map of Africa changed since the Second World War? (See maps, pp. 665, 667, and 927.)

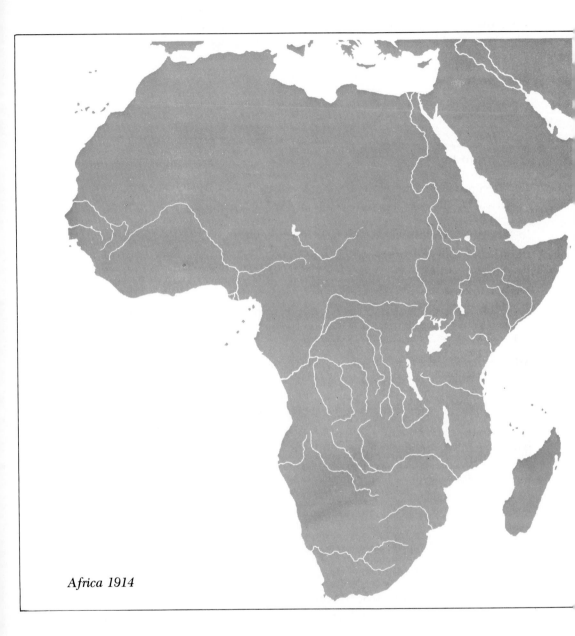

Africa 1914

82. Imperialism in Asia: The Dutch, the British, and the Russians

PICTURE ESSAY: THE BRITISH IN INDIA (pp. 683–693)

Study Questions

1. How did the Dutch create and maintain their empire in the East Indies? What resistance developed?
2. How did British rule in India change after the events of 1857?
3. How would you describe the economy of India under British rule?
4. Explain the growth and nature of Indian nationalism.
5. How do the illustrations and text in the Picture Essay, "The British in India" (pp. 683–693), demonstrate the British social, political, and economic impact on India? How would you assess the balance sheets of the British presence?
6. What seemed to be the principal motives for Russian expansion in Asia? Why and where did the Russians come into conflict with the British?

Key Discussion Sentences

British India and the Dutch East Indies, in the half-century before the First World War, illustrated the kind of empire that all imperialists wished to have.

As nationalism in India grew, it turned against Indian capitalists and took on some of the features of socialism.

Imperial ambitions deepened the hostility between Great Britain and Russia.

Identifications

"culture system"
suttee
sepoys
"Indian Mutiny"
British East India
   Company

Mogul Empire
Empress of India
Indian National
   Congress

All-India Muslim
   League
Afghan wars
partition of Persia

Map Exercise

1. Study the map on p. 671, " 'The British Lake,' 1918." What does the map tell you of the size and extent of the British Empire at its height? Why could the Mediterranean and the Suez Canal be considered the "lifeline" of the empire?

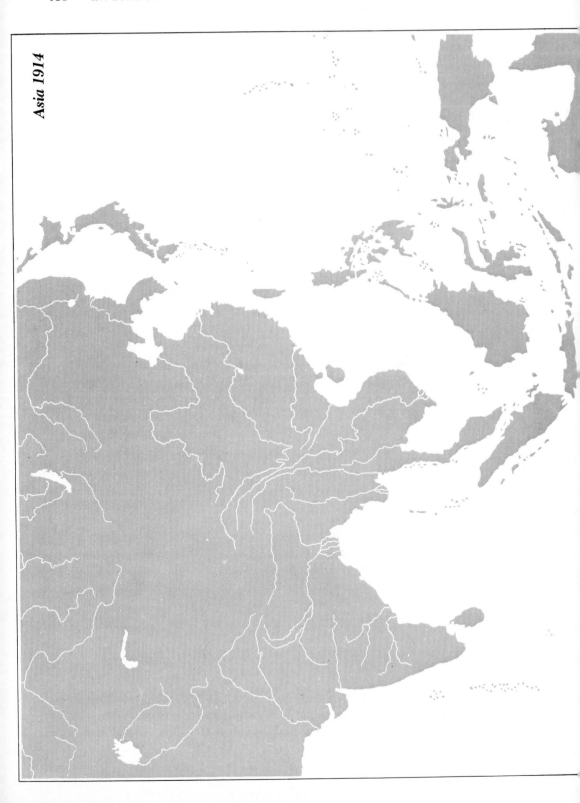

Asia 1914

83. Imperialism in Asia: China and the West

Study Questions

1. What major internal developments were taking place in China in the early nineteenth century? What policy did the Europeans pursue with respect to the Manchu Empire?
2. What rights did Europeans and other outsiders acquire as a result of the Opium Wars? What further gains did Europeans make in China from 1860 to 1898?
3. What did Japan gain as a result of the war with China in 1894? What kind of international crisis followed? Why were the Russians concerned over the status of Manchuria?
4. Summarize the concessions extracted from China in 1898 by the Germans, the Russians, the French, and the British. What were the motives behind the Open Door policy?
5. What were the net consequences of imperialist expansion in China by the end of the nineteenth century?

Key Discussion Sentences

The Manchu dynasty in nineteenth-century China was failing to preserve internal order.

While China was penetrated at the center under the "treaty system," whole slabs of the country were cut away from the outer rim from 1860 to 1898.

The Open Door policy was a program, not so much of leaving China to the Chinese, as of assuring that all outsiders should find it literally "open."

Identifications

Taiping Rebellion	"treaty system"	treaty of Shimonoseki
Opium Wars	extraterritorial rights	Trans-Siberian Railway
burning of the Summer Palace	Annam	Liaotung peninsula
	French Indochina	Open Door
	Sino-Japanese War of 1894	Boxer Rebellion

Map Exercises

1. On the outline map of Asia show the expansion of the foreign powers in Asia by 1914. What gains, territorial and nonterritorial, had been made by each of the major powers by 1914? Suggested source: *A History of the Modern World*, pp. 676–677.
2. Can you locate on this map the places mentioned in Section 83?

84. The Russo-Japanese War and Its Consequences

Study Questions

1. How did the interests of Russia and of Japan conflict in northeast China?
2. Describe the nature and outcome of the Russo-Japanese War. What was President Theodore Roosevelt's objective in his offer of mediation?
3. Of what special significance for later history was the Russo-Japanese War? In what sense did it herald important developments of the twentieth century?

Key Discussion Sentences

It was to the American advantage to have neither Russia nor Japan win too overwhelming a victory in the Far East in 1905.

The Japanese victory and Russian defeat in the Russo-Japanese War can be seen as a prelude to the First World War, the Russian Revolution, and the Revolt of Asia.

Identifications

Chinese Eastern   battle of Mukden   treaty of Portsmouth
  Railway   battle of Tsushima
Anglo-Japanese alliance   Strait

Map Exercise

1. Study the map on p. 679. Why have northeast China and its adjoining regions long been one of the world's trouble zones? Why were both Russia and Japan interested in the area? Of what significance was the area before the First World War? Summarize briefly the status of Manchuria and Korea in the years since the Second World War.

GENERAL ESSAY QUESTIONS FOR CHAPTER XV

1. Why may the years 1870–1914 be considered the years of Europe's world supremacy? What earlier phases of European expansion were there? What developments would end European supremacy?
2. Assess the incentives and motives for nineteenth-century European imperialism. What impact did imperialism have upon non-European peoples (a) in Africa, (b) in Asia? In what sense did the imperialism of 1870–1914 help to create a worldwide civilization?
3. Explain how the imperialist rivalries of the great powers brought them into conflict in the Middle East, Africa, and the Far East. With what results?
4. What may be said of the United States role in the age of imperialism (a) in Latin America, (b) in the Far East?

GENERAL DISCUSSION PASSAGES FOR CHAPTER XV

For the first time in human history, by 1900 it was possible to speak of a world civilization. (p. 643)

European imperialism proved to be transitory, a phase in the worldwide spread of industrial and scientific civilization that had originated in Europe's "inner zone." (p. 643)

In the twentieth century, in opposition to European empires, subject peoples asserted ideas learned from Europe—ideas of liberty and democracy, and of an anticapitalism that passed easily into socialism. (p. 643)

Imperialism arose from the commercial, industrial, financial, scientific, political, journalistic, intellectual, religious, and humanitarian impulses of Europe compounded together. It was an outthrust of the whole white man's civilization. It would bring civilization and enlightened living to those who still sat in darkness. Faith in "modern civilization" had become a kind of substitute religion. Imperialism was its crusade. (p. 650)

In the psychology of imperialism there was much that was not unworthy. It was a good thing to bring clearer ideas of justice to barbaric peoples, to put down slave raiding, torture, and famine, to combat degrading superstitions or fight the diseases of neglect and filth. But these accomplishments, however real, went along too obviously with self-interest and were expressed with unbearable complacency and gross condescension to the larger part of the human race. (p. 650)

As the United States became a great power, the Monroe Doctrine became an effective barrier to European territorial ambitions. Latin America, while exposed to the indignities of dollar diplomacy, never became subject to imperialism as completely as did Asia and Africa. On the other hand, the United States became the imperialist power feared above all others south of the border. It was the *Yanqui* menace, the Colossus of the North. (p. 652)

Under the circumstances of imperialism, everything was done to uproot the Africans, and little was done to benefit them. The old tribal or village society collapsed, and nothing replaced it. (p. 666)

Until the spectacular end of the European empires after the Second World War, the map of Africa remained essentially what the brief years of partition from 1885 to 1900 had made it. (p. 669)

If one examines the results of imperialism in China by about 1900, one can understand how observant Chinese felt at the end of the last century, and why the term "imperialism" came to be held by so many of the world's peoples in abomination. (p. 680)

The moral of the Japanese victory in 1905 was clear. Everywhere leaders of subjugated peoples concluded that they must bring Western science and industry to their own countries, but they must do it, as the Japanese had done, by getting rid of control by the Europeans, supervising the process of modernization themselves, and preserving their own native national character. (p. 682)

The Japanese victory and Russian defeat in 1905 can be seen as steps in three mighty developments: the First World War, the Russian Revolution, and the Revolt of Asia. These three events put an end to Europe's world supremacy and almost to European civilization; or at least they so transmuted them as to make the world of the twentieth century far different from that of the nineteenth. (p. 682)

XVI.
THE FIRST
WORLD WAR
SECTIONS 85–90, pp. 695–731

85. *The International Anarchy*

Study Questions

1. Why were both the French and the British concerned about German aspirations after 1870? What evidence of Anglo-German industrial competition is revealed by the map and chart on p. 699?
2. Explain how the Continent became divided by 1894 into two opposed camps. What developments led the British to abandon their "splendid isolation"?
3. How were European international relations affected in the years 1905 to 1913 by the crises over (a) Morocco and (b) the Balkans?
4. How did the assassination of the Archduke Francis Ferdinand lead to the outbreak of a general European war?
5. How would you assess the responsibility of each of the countries involved in the events of 1914? What role did the alliance system play? other factors?

Key Discussion Sentences

It had long been felt that a unified Germany would revolutionize the relationships of the European peoples; after 1870 these anticipations were more than confirmed.

The Serbs conceived of their small kingdom as the Piedmont of a South Slav Risorgimento.

The Balkan crisis of 1914 proved fatal because two others had gone before it, leaving feelings of exasperation in Austria, desperation in Serbia, and humiliation in Russia.

In a little over a month after the assassination, the chief nations of Europe were locked in combat. It may be argued that each country bore responsibility for the outbreak of the war.

Although it is not true that Germany started the war, as its enemies in 1914 popularly believed, it must be granted that its policies had for some years been rather peremptory, arrogant, devious, and obstinate.

The alliance system was an obvious cause of the war, but it was only a symptom of deeper trouble—the world had an international economy but a national polity.

Identifications

Dual Alliance of 1879	*entente cordiale*	annexation of Bosnia
Triple Alliance	Anglo-Russian	first Balkan War
"reinsurance" treaty	Convention	second Balkan War
Franco-Russian	Triple Entente	South Slavs
Alliance	Tangier incident	Albania
Anglo-Japanese	Agadir crisis	Sarajevo crisis
Alliance	Buchlau conference	German "blank check"

Map Exercise

1. Using the map on p. 703, "The Balkans, 1878 and 1914," locate each of the places mentioned in Section 85.

86. *The Armed Stalemate*

Study Questions

1. What happened to the German Schlieffen Plan when it was put into operation? How did the battle of the Marne affect the character of the war?
2. How would you summarize the major military campaigns of 1915 and 1916? What was the general state of affairs at the end of 1916?
3. What form did the British naval blockade take? German submarine warfare?
4. What success did both sides have in finding new allies in 1914 and 1915? Why did Italy join the Allies?
5. How did each side appeal to discontented nationalist groups? Why could the Allies be more successful?
6. Why may it be said that the war accelerated prewar imperialist tendencies? In what sense was this true of the Allies? What expansionist aims did the Germans reveal?
7. How would you describe President Wilson's attitude toward the war and toward the two opposing alliances in the early years of the war?

Key Discussion Sentences

After the failure of the Schlieffen Plan the war of movement in the West settled into a war of position.

To the Allies a long war gave many advantages.

The submarine was an unrefined weapon.

Each side tampered with minorities and discontented groups living within the other's domain.

The war aims of the Germans were even more expansionist than those of the Allies.

Although his personal sympathies lay with England and France, Woodrow Wilson saw little difference between the warring alliances.

Identifications

Central Powers	"they shall not pass"	Sir Roger Casement
Moltke	battle of the Somme	Zimmermann telegram
Joffre	sinking of the *Lusitania*	Balfour note of 1917
battle of Tannenberg	battle of Jutland	Armenian deportations
Dardanelles campaign	secret treaty of London	Twenty-One Demands
battle of Verdun	of 1915	Bethmann-Hollweg

Map Exercises

1. What does the map on p. 705 reveal about the nature of the land fighting in the First World War?
2. Can you locate each of the places mentioned in Section 86?

87. The Collapse of Russia and the Intervention of the United States

Study Questions

1. What effect did revolutionary events in Russia in 1917 have on the First World War? Explain the significance of the treaty of Brest-Litovsk.
2. Why did President Wilson change his opinion of the war? Why did he call for American entry?
3. How successful was the German submarine campaign in 1917? the counter-measures adopted to meet it?
4. Describe the nature and outcome (a) of the military campaigns on the Western Front in 1917 and (b) of the German offensive in the West in the spring of 1918. What were the results of the Allied offensive?
5. How did the casualties of the United States compare with those of the other combatants? What is suggested as the major significance of American participation in the war?

Key Discussion Sentences

The treaty of Brest-Litovsk represented the maximum success of the Germans during the First World War.

Having made his decision that Germany was a menace, Wilson now saw a clear-cut issue between right and wrong.

American assistance came so late, when the others had been struggling for so long, that the mere beginnings of it were enough to turn the scale.

Identifications

treaty of Brest-Litovsk	Nivelle	Caporetto
Hindenburg	Pétain	Foch
Ludendorff	Passchendaele	

Map Exercise

1. Using the map on p. 705, locate each of the places mentioned in recounting the events of 1917 and 1918.

88. *The Collapse of the Austrian and German Empires*

Study Questions

1. What happened to the Austro-Hungarian Empire at the close of the war?
2. Explain the position taken by Ludendorff and the German High Command in the autumn of 1918. What governmental and constitutional changes did they insist upon?
3. Describe the background to the abdication of the Kaiser. How "revolutionary" were these events?

Key Discussion Sentences

The war proved fatal to the German and Austro-Hungarian Empires as well as to the Russian Empire.

It was untrue that Germany had been "stabbed in the back" by a dissolving civilian home front.

89. *The Economic and Social Impact of the War*

Study Questions

1. What impact did the First World War have upon private enterprise and the economy? In what specific ways did wartime governments control economic

activities? What special measures of economic control were adopted by Germany? by the Allied countries?

2. What were the short- and long-run effects of government wartime monetary policies? Of what significance were the national debts that were created?

3. How did the war change the economic and financial status of the United States? How did the war affect the industrialization of countries outside Europe?

4. What effect did the war have on the entry of women into the labor force?

5. To what extent did governments during the war attempt to control ideas? With what consequences?

Key Discussion Sentences

The idea of the "planned economy" was first applied in the First World War.

In Germany, government controls became more thorough and more efficient than elsewhere.

With Europe torn by war for four years, the rest of the world speeded up its own industrialization.

During the war, freedom of thought, respected for half a century, was discarded.

90. The Peace of Paris, 1919

Study Questions

1. On what principles did Woodrow Wilson desire peace to be established? Why did he hope for a new kind of peace settlement?

2. Describe the personality and political outlook of the other Big Four statesmen. Why did Wilson and Lloyd George object to the French attitudes and proposals with respect to Germany?

3. Summarize and discuss the major agreements reached at the peace conference concerning (a) territorial changes, (b) disposition of the German colonies, (c) restrictions on German naval and military power, (d) reparations.

4. Why was the "war guilt" clause written into the treaty? What objections might legitimately be raised to it?

5. How did the war and the peace treaties change the political structure of Europe? What is meant by the *cordon sanitaire*?

6. How would you evaluate the success and the wisdom of the treaty of Versailles? What sources of future trouble might be anticipated?

Key Discussion Sentences

To obtain a League of Nations, Wilson made a number of concessions and compromised the idealism of the Fourteen Points.

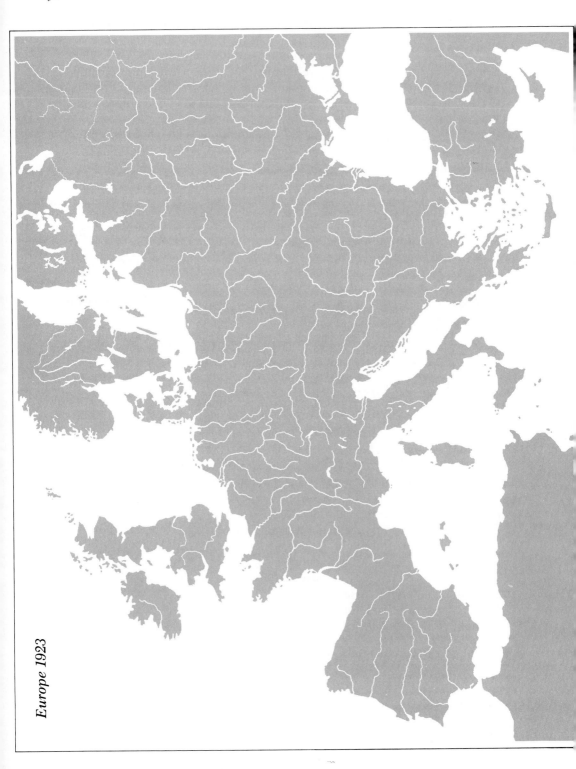

Europe 1923

The Germans felt no such responsibility for the war as they were obliged formally to accept under the "war guilt" clause.

The most general principle of the Paris settlement was to recognize the right of national self-determination, at least in Europe.

For practical purposes the treaty of Versailles, with respect to Germany, was either too severe or too lenient.

The League of Nations marked a great step beyond the international anarchy before 1914, but it had its limitations.

The war was indeed a victory for democracy, though a bitter one.

Identifications

Lloyd George
Clemenceau
Orlando
Fourteen Points
Anglo-French-
  American treaty

demilitarization of the
  Rhineland
the Saar
Sudeten Germans
"mandates"
Polish Corridor

Kingdom of the Serbs,
  Croats, and Slovenes
reparations
"war guilt" clause
League of Nations
  covenant

Map Exercises

1. On the outline map of Europe show Europe's political boundaries in 1923 after the Paris peace settlement of 1919 and other postwar settlements. How does this map of Europe differ from the one of Europe in 1914? How closely does it conform to the distribution of language groups in Europe? Suggested source: *A History of the Modern World*, pp. 470, 562–563, and 728–729.
2. Can you locate each of the places mentioned in Section 90?

GENERAL ESSAY QUESTIONS FOR CHAPTER XVI

1. What general political and economic circumstances contributed to the outbreak of war in 1914? How did the assassination of the Archduke Francis Ferdinand lead to a European-wide war in so short a period of time? How would you assess the responsibility of each of the great powers for the outbreak of the war?
2. In what ways did the First World War affect the European economy and European society?
3. In what sense did Woodrow Wilson hope to arrive at a treaty that would be different from earlier diplomatic efforts? How successful was he? What obstacles did he encounter?
4. "The wisdom of the treaty of Versailles has been discussed without end." Debate (a) the strengths and weaknesses of the treaty, (b) the "wisdom" or lack of wisdom of the treaty.

GENERAL DISCUSSION PASSAGES FOR CHAPTER XVI

Somewhere before 1914 Europe went off its course. Europeans believed themselves to be heading for a kind of high plateau, full of a benign progress and more abundant civilization. Instead, Europe stumbled in 1914 into disaster. (p. 695)

In the last years before 1914, the idea that war was bound to break out sooner or later probably made some statesmen in some countries more willing to unleash it. (p. 696)

The reformer who makes a system work is the most dangerous of all enemies to the implacable revolutionary, and it is perhaps for this reason that Archduke Francis Ferdinand was assassinated. (p. 702)

The world had an international economy but a national polity. There was no world state to police the worldwide system, assuring participation in the world economy to all nations under all conditions. (pp. 704–705)

In a world that was in the strict sense anarchic (and seemed likely to remain so), the alliances were a means by which each nation attempted to bolster its security. (p. 706)

Western Europe's position as the world's workshop was undermined by the First World War. The age of European supremacy was in its twilight. (pp. 721–722)

Woodrow Wilson stood for the fruition of the democratic, liberal, progressive, and nationalist movements of the century past, as well as for the ideals of the Enlightenment, of the French Revolution, and of 1848. (p. 723)

The circumstances under which the German republic originated in 1918 made its later history, and hence all later history, very troubled. (p. 718)

The First World War forced European society into many basic changes that were to prove more lasting than the war itself. (p. 718)

The war gave a new impetus even to the idea of economic equality, if only to enlist rich and poor alike in a common cause. (p. 719)

The wartime experience in the First and Second World Wars, in which women took over many jobs which it had been thought only men could do, was part of the process by which the labor force in all countries was enlarged, women's place in society revolutionized, and the lives and outlook of millions of individual women turned outward from the home. (p. 719)

There was thought to be something sinister about peace conferences of the past. The old diplomacy was blamed for leading to war. It was felt that treaties had too long been wrongly based on a politics of power or on unprincipled deals and bargains made without regard to the people concerned. (p. 723)

In his own way and for his own purposes, Lenin, like Wilson, condemned the old diplomacy. (p. 723)

Nationalism triumphed at the Paris peace conference in the belief that it went along naturally with liberalism and democracy. (p. 727)

The First World War was indeed a victory for democracy, though a bitter one. It furthered a process as old as the French and American Revolutions. But for the basic problems of modern civilization, industrialism and nationalism, economic security and international stability, it gave no answer. (p. 731)

XVII.
THE RUSSIAN
REVOLUTION
AND THE
SOVIET UNION
SECTIONS 91–96, pp. 732–776

91. Backgrounds

Study Questions

1. What reforms had been introduced in Russia under Alexander II? What policies did Alexander III pursue? With what results?
2. How did industrialization in the closing decades of the nineteenth century affect (a) the wage-earning class, (b) the capitalist class?
3. What special features characterized land ownership and the agrarian economy in Russia?
4. How did the Social Revolutionary party differ in attitudes and program from the Social Democratic Labor party?
5. Describe Lenin's personality and background. How would you evaluate his contributions to Marxism? What special factors in the Russian background affected his conception of a revolutionary party and of revolution?

Key Discussion Sentences

In the closing decades of the nineteenth century, Russia became more than ever before a part of European civilization.

The populists had a mystical faith in the Russian peasantry.

The Russian Marxists believed that Russia must develop capitalism before there could be any revolution.

Bolshevism, or Leninism, differed from Menshevism on the nature of the party and on its relationship to other political groups.

Lenin reaffirmed Marx's basic analysis of society, reinforced certain theories of imperialism, and expanded on Marx's ideas on the role of the party.

Identifications

pogrom	*mir*	Social Democratic
Russification	Social Revolutionary	Labor party
Pobiedonostsev	party	Bolsheviks
Count Witte	Plekhanov	Mensheviks
Constitutional	Axelrod	Leninism
Democrats		

92. *The Revolution of 1905*

Study Questions

1. What signs of dissatisfaction could be discerned in Russia at the opening of the twentieth century? Of what significance was the war with Japan?
2. Describe the background and nature of the Revolution of 1905. What precipitated the revolution? With what consequences?
3. What appeared to be the chief result of the Revolution of 1905? What actually was the result?
4. Explain the objectives and accomplishments of Stolypin. What sources of discontent persisted in the countryside despite his reforms?
5. In what direction did Russia seem to be moving by 1914?

Key Discussion Sentences

At the turn of the century, the almost simultaneous founding of three parties—the Constitutional Democrats, the Social Revolutionaries, and the Social Democrats—was clearly a sign of mounting dissatisfaction.

Tsar Nicholas II regarded the mildest liberalism or democracy as un-Russian.

The one thing that tsarism would not allow, even after 1905, was any real participation in the government by the people.

Although still violent and half barbaric, the Russian Empire on the eve of the First World War seemed to be developing according to a Western pattern.

Identifications

Nicholas II	"soviets"	Duma
Father Gapon	St. Petersburg Soviet	"Cadets"
"Bloody Sunday"	October Manifesto	

93. *The Revolution of 1917*

Study Questions

1. Why did dissatisfaction with the wartime tsarist regime emerge?
2. How was the crisis of March 1917 precipitated? What revolutionary events followed?
3. Describe the program of the Provisional Government and the obstacles it faced.
4. Explain the appeal of Lenin's program. Under what circumstances did the Bolsheviks seize power? Describe the new machinery of government.
5. What action did Lenin take with respect to the war? Why did he accept the Brest-Litovsk treaty?
6. In what sense was "war communism" a "mixture of principle and expediency"? How did these policies lead to trouble with the peasants?
7. Which groups resisted the new regime in the civil war? What role did the Allied governments play? What factors helped the Bolsheviks to triumph?
8. How might the Terror in Russia be compared with the Terror of the French Revolution? What were the net results of the Terror and civil war?

Key Discussion Sentences

The war put the tsarist regime to a test that it could not meet.

Lenin and the Bolsheviks did not bring about the Russian Revolution. They captured it after it had begun. They boarded the ship in midstream.

Lenin and the Bolsheviks called for "Peace, land, and bread" and for "All power to the Soviets!"

Lenin's dissolution of the Constituent Assembly revealed the Bolshevik attitude toward political democracy.

By the peace of Brest-Litovsk with Germany, the Bolsheviks abandoned the Russian conquests of two centuries.

The anti-Communist Russians represented every hue of the political spectrum.

The Red Army reconquered those areas of the tsarist empire which had declared their independence.

The Terror succeeded in its purpose.

Identifications

Rasputin	General Kornilov	treaty of Brest-Litovsk
Duma executive committee	Constituent Assembly	Cheka
Petrograd Soviet	November (or October) Revolution	Red Army
		Leon Trotsky

March (or February)
  Revolution
Provisional
  Government
Prince Lvov
Alexander Kerensky

Congress of Soviets
Council of People's
  Commissars

White armies
Kronstadt mutiny
Azerbaijan
Admiral Kolchak

Map Exercises

1. Study the maps on pp. 242–243, 728–729, and 758–759. Describe the territorial losses of Russia from 1918 to 1922. Explain this statement: "Russia had lost thousands of square miles of territory and buffer areas acquired over the centuries by the tsars. They remained lost until the Second World War." (P. 753; see also pp. 754–755.)
2. Can you locate and describe the areas of the tsarist empire that declared their independence and were reconquered by the Red Army? (See p. 752 and map, pp. 758–759.)

94. The Union of Soviet Socialist Republics

Study Questions

1. Why was the problem of nationalities important in Russia? How did the tsarist regime attempt to deal with it?
2. Describe the Soviet response to the nationalities problem (a) in theory and (b) in practice.
3. Describe governmental institutions and the suffrage in the Soviet Union before 1936. What changes were made in 1936?
4. What link was there between party and government in the Soviet Union? How were decisions arrived at in the party? In what sense did the party tend to lose its original character?
5. Explain the background, nature, and results of the New Economic Policy.
6. What role did Stalin play in the struggle for power that took place in the years immediately following Lenin's death? What criticisms did Trotsky level at the Soviet regime in 1925–1926?

Key Discussion Sentences

The federal principle in the U.S.S.R. was designed to answer the problem of the nationalities.

In theory a principle of parallelism for state and party was adopted in the Soviet Union.

The party in the U.S.S.R. functioned as a highly disciplined leadership group.

The New Economic Policy, which lasted from 1921 to 1927, represented a compromise with capitalism.

Identifications

soviet republics	Council of People's	Politburo
Russian S.F.S.R.	Commissars	*kulak*
Supreme Soviet	Central Committee	"permanent
Soviet of Nationalities	General Secretary	revolution"

Map Exercise

1. Study the map on pp. 758–759 and the tables, pp. 754 and 1016. What do they tell you about the multinational nature of the U.S.S.R.? What other information may be derived from the two tables? Can you locate the Soviet republics listed on p. 754? (See map, pp. 758–759.)

95. Stalin: The Five-Year Plans and the Purges

Study Questions

1. What ideas and precedents contributed to the concept of economic planning?
2. Explain the objectives of the First Five-Year Plan and the system established to carry it out.
3. Explain the origins and nature of the collectivization program in agriculture. At what cost was it accomplished? How would you summarize its net results?
4. What generalizations may be made about the growth of industry and of production under the Five-Year plans? Explain the qualifications that must be made about Soviet industrial growth. What conclusions for both industry and agriculture may be drawn from the chart on p. 769?
5. How would you evaluate the effects of the Five-Year plans on Soviet society? To what extent was economic equality realized or sought? What kind of competition persisted?
6. Describe the purges and purge trials of the 1930s. What was their net result?

Key Discussion Sentences

Economic planning became the distinctive feature of Soviet economics.

No ten years in the history of any Western country ever showed such a rate of industrial growth as the decade of the first two Five-Year plans in the Soviet Union.

The year 1929, not 1917, was the great revolutionary year for most people in Russia.

Collectivization of agriculture was to make possible the success of industrialization.

The degree of industrialization in the U.S.S.R. can easily be exaggerated.

Solidarity in the U.S.S.R. was purchased at the price of totalitarianism.

Identifications

First Five-Year Plan	Machine Tractor	Kirov
Gosplan	Stations	Trotskyists
collective farm	Second Five-Year Plan	"rightists"
liquidation of the	Stakhanovite	Bukharin
kulaks	constitution of 1936	purges and purge trials
		Marshal Tukhachevski

Map Exercises

1. Study the map on pp. 758–759 and the accompanying caption. What observations may be made about the outstanding geographical features of the U.S.S.R.?
2. Can you locate each of the places mentioned in Section 95 in connection with the Five-Year plans?

96. The International Impact of Communism, 1919–1939

Study Questions

1. How was international socialism affected (a) by the First World War and (b) by the Russian Revolution?
2. What events led to the founding of the Third International? What role did the Russian party play in its creation and operation?
3. Explain the stages through which the Comintern passed in the years following its inception.

Key Discussion Sentences

In the First World War the working class in every Western country proved its national loyalty.

The mass of European socialists remained wedded to gradual, peaceable, and parliamentary methods.

Lenin believed that the Russian Revolution was only a local phase of a world revolution.

It was not through the Comintern that the U.S.S.R. exerted its greatest influence.

Identifications

revisionism	Spartacist movement	Zinoviev
Zimmerwald program	Béla Kun	Twenty-One Points
Zimmerwald Left	First International	"popular fronts"
Social Democrats	Second International	Third International

GENERAL ESSAY QUESTIONS FOR CHAPTER XVII

1. How would you compare the Russian Revolution of 1917 with the French Revolution of 1789? What similarities and differences need to be stressed?
2. In what sense is it accurate to say that Lenin and the Bolsheviks did not "cause" the Russian Revolution but captured it after it had begun? How would you compare the two revolutions in Russia in the year 1917?
3. In what direction did Russia seem to be heading economically on the eve of the First World War? What was the Soviet economy like on the eve of the Second World War? How did this come about? What weaknesses were there in the economy?
4. Discuss the international impact of the Russian Revolution from 1917 to the Second World War. What special appeal did it have in various parts of the world? How did it lose its claim to leadership of oppressed peoples?

GENERAL DISCUSSION PASSAGES FOR CHAPTER XVII

No less powerful than the First World War as a force shaping the twentieth century has been the Russian Revolution of 1917. (p. 696)

The Russian Revolution of 1917 can be compared in its magnitude only with the French Revolution of 1789. Both made their repercussions felt in many countries for many years. The similarities and differences are equally striking. (pp. 732–733)

The Russian Revolution, like all great revolutions, originated in a totality of previous history and in the prolonged dissatisfaction of many kinds of people. (p. 734)

The Russian Revolution not only produced communism and hence fascism in Europe, but it also added strength to the revolt of Asia. (p. 734)

One traditional source of revolutionary disturbance in old Russia lay among the intelligentsia. In the kind of society that Russia was under the tsars, many of the best and purest spirits were attracted to violence and yearned for a catastrophic overthrow of the tsardom. (p. 737)

Genius has been called the faculty for everlasting concentration on one thing. For Lenin this thing was revolution. (p. 738)

Lenin accomplished the marriage of Russian revolutionary traditions with the Western doctrine of Marxism. It was an improbable marriage, whose momentous offspring was communism. (p. 741)

"Planning," or the central planning of a country's whole economic life by government officials, was to become the distinctive feature of Soviet economics and the one that, for a time, was to have the greatest influence on the rest of the world. (p. 762)

How the confessions of the Old Bolsheviks were obtained in open court, from men apparently in full possession of their faculties and bearing no sign of physical harm, long mystified the outside world. (p. 771)

For Communists, though not for socialists, the terms "communism" and "socialism" were almost interchangeable. (p. 761)

Of all enemies the Communists hated the socialists most, reserving for them even choicer epithets than they bestowed upon capitalists and imperialists. (p. 774)

By 1939 the U.S.S.R. exerted its influence on the world by the massive fact of its very existence. It was clear that a new type of economic system had been created, embracing a sixth of the globe, which called itself Marxist. (pp. 775–776)

In the 1930s some believed or hoped that something like Soviet results might be obtained without the use of Soviet methods. (p. 776)

The so-called backward peoples, especially in Asia, were particularly impressed by the achievement of the U.S.S.R., which had shown how a traditional society could modernize itself without falling under the influence of foreign capital or foreign guidance. (p. 776)

In later years it became problematic whether the Soviets could prevent the disintegration of their multinational state. (p. 756)

With the passage of time and its historical record, it became impossible for the U.S.S.R. to present itself as the leader of world revolution and of oppressed peoples elsewhere, or exert control over other Communist parties. (p. 776)

XVIII.
THE
APPARENT
VICTORY OF
DEMOCRACY
SECTIONS 97–100, pp. 777–804

97. *The Advance of Democracy after 1919*

Study Questions

1. What evidence of the advance of political democracy was observable in the early postwar years? What trend in social legislation?
2. Why may the new states that emerged after 1919 be called accidents of the war? With what major problems did they have to contend?
3. Describe (a) the economic steps taken by the new states of central and eastern Europe to modernize themselves and (b) the land reforms initiated. What were the results in each case?

Key Discussion Sentences

Democracy made advances after 1919 even in democratic countries.

A democratic innovation after 1919 was the enfranchisement of women.

The welfare state became more firmly established after the First World War.

Economically, the carving up of eastern Europe was self-defeating.

Each of the new successor states included minority nationalities.

Map Exercise

1. Study the map of Europe in 1923 on pp. 728–729. Locate the new successor states after 1919 and indicate the pre-1914 empires from which they had emerged. What minority problems might be anticipated?

98. *The German Republic and the Spirit of Locarno*

Study Questions

1. What may be said about the revolution in Germany in 1918? How profound were the changes introduced?
2. Assess the role played by the German Social Democrats in the early years of the Weimar Republic.
3. What threats to the republic arose from the left? from the right? What persistent problems did the republic face?
4. How did the French attitude toward reparations lead to the Ruhr episode of 1923? With what results?
5. What circumstances brought Germany and Russia together? With what results?
6. How did the great inflation of 1923 affect the various classes in Germany?
7. How were fundamental issues of international affairs being met in the 1920s? What was the nature and significance of Locarno?

Key Discussion Sentences

The Weimar Republic, of which the Social Democrats were the main architects in its formative years, was remote from anything socialistic.

No one in Germany, not even the Social Democrats, accepted the treaty of Versailles or the new German frontiers as either just or final.

The German inflation of 1923 brought far more of a social revolution than had the fall of the Hohenzollern empire.

The treaties signed at Locarno marked the highest point of international good will reached between the two world wars.

Identifications

German Social Democratic party	treaty of Rapallo	Dawes Plan
Spartacist uprising	occupation of the Ruhr	Kellogg-Briand Pact
Weimar Republic	war debts	Rosa Luxemburg
Kapp *Putsch*	reparations	Gustav Stresemann

99. *The Revolt of Asia*

Study Questions

1. How did aroused and self-conscious Asians view imperialism? With what justification?
2. How did each of the following affect twentieth-century developments in Asia:

(a) the Russo-Japanese War, (b) the First World War, (c) the Russian Revolution?

3. Explain the nature and results of the Turkish Revolution. What sweeping changes were introduced? What similar developments took place in Iran?

4. What major developments occurred in the Indian independence movement in the twenty years between the two world wars? Explain the differences in attitudes that developed among the Indian nationalists.

5. Describe the background, career, and program of Sun Yat-sen. Why did Sun cooperate with Russia and the Chinese Communists? With what results?

6. What success did the Kuomintang armies have between 1924 and 1928? What caused the rift between the Kuomintang and the Communists?

7. Explain the changes taking place in Japanese political life in the 1920s. Of what significance for international affairs was the Japanese invasion of Manchuria?

Key Discussion Sentences

The Revolt of Asia was a revolt against Western supremacy, but at the same time those who revolted meant to learn from and imitate the West.

Nationalism in Asia easily shaded off into socialism and a denunciation of capitalist exploitation.

In Turkey, Mustapha Kemal put through a sweeping revolution.

In the Turkish Revolution, for the first time in any Islamic country, the spheres of government and religion were sharply distinguished.

The ideas of the Chinese Revolution were best expressed by Sun Yat-sen's three principles of the people—democracy, nationalism, and livelihood.

In 1931 the League of Nations failed to prevent open and undisguised aggression in Manchuria.

Identifications

Baku congress
Atatürk
Reza Khan
Iran
Indian National
    Congress
Mohandas K. Gandhi
Jawaharlal Nehru

Yuan Shih-kai
Kuomintang
*The Three People's
    Principles*
May Fourth movement
Chiang Kai-shek

Borodin
war lords
the Long March
Mao Tse-tung
Zaibatsu
Lytton Commission

Map Exercise

1. Study the maps of Asia on pp. 676–677 and on the back end papers. Can you locate each of the places mentioned in Section 99?

100. *The Great Depression: Collapse of the World Economy*

Study Questions

1. Explain the major weaknesses in the prosperity of the 1920s.
2. What brought on the stock market crash of October 1929? Describe the events that followed the financial crisis.
3. Explain the impact of the depression on the world economy.
4. How did the unemployment crisis affect people? political developments?
5. What explanations for the depression were offered? What might be said in favor of each view?
6. Describe the economic measures taken by governments during the depression. How did these measures affect the world economy?

Key Discussion Sentences

The capitalist economic system was a delicate and interlocking mechanism. Any disturbance was rapidly transmitted through all its parts.

In the 1920s a great deal of production was financed by credit, and the whole system rested, to a large extent, upon mutual confidence and mutual exchange.

The crisis passed from finance to industry, and from the United States to the rest of the world.

Optimists declared that the depression was merely a phase in the business cycle. Others felt that it represented the breakdown of the whole system of capitalism.

The most marked consequence of the depression was a movement toward economic nationalism.

Identifications

"margin"	"flight from the	Ottawa agreements
Creditanstalt	pound"	
	Hawley-Smoot tariff	

GENERAL ESSAY QUESTIONS FOR CHAPTER XVIII

1. How would you characterize the 1920s from the point of view of (a) the international economy, (b) domestic affairs, (c) international affairs?
2. What impact did the Great Depression have on the world economy? Why did it lead to a resurgence of economic nationalism?
3. In what sense was the "Revolt of Asia" a revolt against the age of imperialism? What special form did it take in the interwar years in (a) Turkey, (b) Iran, (c) India, (d) China? With what results?

GENERAL DISCUSSION PASSAGES FOR CHAPTER XVIII

From the formal close of the First World War in 1919 to the outbreak of the Second World War in 1939, the world made a dizzy passage from confidence to disillusionment and from hope to fear. (p. 777)

Germany, too, had its revolution in 1918. But it was a revolution without revolutionaries, a negative revolution caused more by the disappearance of the old than by any vehement arrival of the new. There had in truth been no revolution at all, in the sense in which France, England, the United States, Russia, and other countries, either recently or in the more distant past, had experienced revolutions. (pp. 783, 784)

The middle, in politics, is an awkward spot, especially in disturbed times. (p. 783)

After the catastrophic inflation of 1923 in Germany, middle-class people were materially in much the position of day laborers and proletarians. Their whole view of life, however, made it impossible for them to identify themselves with the laboring class or to accept its Marxist or socialist ideologies. (p. 786)

The peoples of Asia had never been satisfied with the position in which the great European expansion of the nineteenth century had placed them. In deeper psychology, as well as in economics, culture, and politics, the revolt of self-conscious Asians was a rebellion against social inferiority and humiliation. (p. 789)

In Marxist-Leninist ideology, imperialism was an aspect of capitalism. Colonial peoples also tended to identify the two, not so much for Marxist reasons as because modern capitalism was a foreign or ''imperialist'' phenomenon in colonial countries, where the ownership and the management of large enterprises were both foreign. (p. 790)

The postwar situation in Asia was extremely fluid. People who were not Communists hailed communism as a liberating force. Anti-Westerners declared that their countries must westernize. Nationalism overshadowed all other ''isms.'' Rich capitalists consorted with socialist leaders and worked in relative harmony so long as there was a common enemy. (p. 791)

For a people wishing to raise itself by its own bootstraps, to move from poverty to industrial strength and higher living standards without loss of time and without dependence on foreign capital and capitalism, the Soviet Union, with its economic planning, seemed to offer a more appropriate model and more practical lessons than the rich democracies of the West, with their centuries of gradual progress behind them. (p. 794)

Never had there been such waste as in the Great Depression, not merely of machinery which now stood still, but of the trained and disciplined labor force on which all modern societies were built. And people chronically out of work naturally turned to new and disturbing political ideas. (p. 802)

The Great Depression put an end to the old economic system. Even if such a stricken economy had internal powers of full recuperation after a few years, people would not stand for such terrifying insecurity in their personal lives. (p. 802)

The era that had opened with Woodrow Wilson's dream of international economic cooperation ended with an unprecedented intensification of economic rivalry and national self-centeredness. It was only one of the promises of the post-1919 world to be blasted by the Great Depression. (p. 804)

XIX. DEMOCRACY AND DICTATORSHIP

SECTIONS 101–104,
pp. 805–833

101. The United States: Depression and New Deal

Study Questions

1. Under what circumstances was Franklin D. Roosevelt elected president? How had President Hoover attempted to cope with the depression?
2. What is meant by the New Deal? Summarize the short-range and longer-range measures adopted.
3. To what extent was economic recovery achieved under the New Deal? What general economic philosophy did it seem to follow?
4. What conclusions may be reached about the nature and significance of the New Deal?

Key Discussion Sentences

Although not following any consistent economic philosophy, New Deal policies indirectly reflected the economic theories of Keynes.

After 1935 the New Deal seemed to shift more and more toward an emphasis on regulation and reform.

The New Deal transformed the noninterventionist state into a welfare or social service state.

The New Deal aimed not at destroying the system of capitalism but at reviving it.

Identifications

National Recovery
   Administration
"deficit financing"
Social Security Act
Fair Labor Standards
   Act

*The General Theory of
   Employment,
   Interest, and Money*
National Labor Rela-
   tions (Wagner) Act
AFL
CIO

Securities and
   Exchange Com-
   mission
Tennessee Valley
   Authority
recession
"Roosevelt
   Revolution"

102. *Trials and Adjustments of Democracy in Britain and France*

Study Questions

1. Explain the circumstances that contributed to Britain's economic difficulties in the twentieth century. How were these difficulties reflected in the events of the 1920s?
2. What explanations are possible for the emergence of the Labour party as one of Britain's two major parties in the years after 1922?
3. Analyze the impact of the depression on Britain. How did the Labour government of 1929 become transformed into a National government?
4. How did the National government attempt to cope with the depression? How successful was it? What might be said about British representative institutions in the crisis of the 1930s?
5. How successfully did the British cope with the problems of the empire? with the Commonwealth? with the Irish question?
6. With what issues was France preoccupied in the 1920s? What were economic conditions like? How did the depression affect France economically?
7. Under what circumstances did the Popular Front emerge in France? How did it resemble and differ from the American New Deal?

Key Discussion Sentences

Britain, like the United States, remained firmly attached to representative institutions and democratic principles, even during the troubles of the depression.

The Great Depression aggravated and intensified Britain's older economic difficulties, which dated back to the years before 1914.

The Popular Front ministry put through a program of legislation unprecedented in French parliamentary annals.

As a result of the Popular Front, internal divisions and class hatreds grew sharper, but the Third Republic was preserved.

The economic destiny of Europeans in the 1930s was very much in doubt.

Identifications

dole	Ramsay MacDonald	Raymond Poincaré
general strike of 1926	Sinn Fein party	Stavisky riots
Trades Disputes Act of 1927	Statute of Westminster	French Popular Front
	Radical Socialists	Léon Blum
Zinoviev letter		

103. *Italian Fascism*

Study Questions

1. What elements of dissatisfaction and unrest appeared in Italy after the First World War? How did Mussolini and the Fascists take advantage of the postwar situation?
2. Describe the regime that Mussolini established. What was the purpose, in theory, of the corporative state? What was it actually like?
3. What arguments were advanced to assert the superiority of fascism and the corporative state over Western democracy?
4. How would you evaluate the accomplishments and failures of the Fascist regime?

Key Discussion Sentences

The corporative state was the Fascist answer to Western-style democracy and to Soviet proletarian dictatorship. Fascism, said Mussolini, is the "dictatorship of the state over many classes cooperating."

Fascism failed to provide either the economic security or the material well-being for which it had demanded the sacrifice of individual freedom.

In other countries fascism came to be regarded as a possible alternative to democratic or parliamentary government and a corrective for troubles whose reality no one could deny.

Identifications

fascio di combattimento	*squadristi*	corporative state
Blackshirts	Matteotti	Chamber of Fasces and
fascism	*Duce*	Corporations
"March on Rome"		

104. *Totalitarianism: Germany's Third Reich*

Study Questions

1. Explain the problems with which the Weimar Republic had to contend in its early years.
2. What attitudes did Hitler form in Vienna before the First World War? What role did the war play in his life? How would you describe the message of *Mein Kampf?*
3. How did the Great Depression affect Germany? How did Hitler exploit the feelings generated in Germany by the Great Depression?

4. Describe the circumstances under which Hitler became chancellor. Of what significance were the months from June 1932 to January 1933? the elections of March 1933?
5. Explain the outstanding political, economic, and social changes introduced in Germany under the Third Reich. Was the Nazi revolution truly a revolution?
6. In what sense was the twentieth-century totalitarian state an outgrowth of the past? How did it differ from political phenomena of the past?

Key Discussion Sentences

Without the Great Depression, Adolf Hitler might have faded out of history.

Democracy, in Germany, could easily be attacked as an imported doctrine.

In anti-Semitism Hitler found a lowest common denominator upon which to appeal to all parties and classes.

Hitler became chancellor by entirely legal means.

All institutions were "coordinated" under the new regime.

The trend to dictatorship or totalitarianism spread over Europe in the 1930s.

Totalitarianism must be distinguished from mere dictatorship.

Identifications

Nazis	Nationalist party	Nuremberg laws
Munich "beer hall *Putsch*"	Franz von Papen	purge of 1934
	Reichstag fire	Gestapo
Kurt von Schleicher	Third Reich	National Labor Front
Paul von Hindenburg	Aryan	Strength Through Joy

GENERAL ESSAY QUESTIONS FOR CHAPTER XIX

1. How did the general mood of the 1930s compare with the mood of the 1920s? What developments brought about the change? What accounted for the setbacks to democracy in many parts of Europe?
2. Why have the 1930s been characterized as the "painful decade"?
3. Compare the political response to the Great Depression in (a) the United States, (b) Britain, (c) France, (d) Germany. How successfully did each cope with the economic collapse?
4. Compare and contrast Italian Fascism and German National Socialism in as many ways as you can, examining the origins, nature, and consequences of each.
5. What is meant generically by "fascism"? by "totalitarianism"? How did the Soviet regime resemble and differ from other dictatorships?

GENERAL DISCUSSION PASSAGES FOR CHAPTER XIX

In the 1920s, people in a general way believed that the twentieth century was realizing all those goals summed up in the idea of progress. In the 1930s they began to fear that progress was a phantom. They began to speak the word self-consciously with mental quotation marks, and to be content if only they could prevent a relapse into positive barbarization and a new world war. (p. 805)

The Great Depression ushered in the nightmare of the 1930s. Where democratic institutions were strong and resilient, governments remained democratically controlled but assumed heavy new social responsibilities. On the other hand, where democratic governments were not well established or taken for granted, dictatorship spread alarmingly in the 1930s. (p. 805)

Unorthodox as "deficit financing" was, it seemed to many at the time the only direct and rapid method of preventing economic collapse in a capitalist system. (p. 808)

If the New Deal did not strike at the deeper roots of American poverty, urban decay, and racial discrimination, it at least demonstrated that the national community cared, and it showed the enormous potential for government action along those fronts. (p. 809)

Totalitarianism, unlike dictatorship, was not merely a theory of government but a theory of life and of human nature. (p. 818)

As time passed, Soviet totalitarianism, though different in many theoretical aspects, became harder to distinguish from other forms of totalitarianism. (p. 828)

The avowed philosophy of totalitarian regimes was subjective. Whether an idea was held to be true depended on whose idea it was. (p. 829)

With totalitarianism the older concepts of reason, natural law, natural right, and the ultimate alikeness of all mankind, or of a common path of all mankind in one course of progress, disappeared. (pp. 829–830)

Totalitarianism was an escape from the realities of class conflict. It was a way of pretending that differences between rich and poor were of minor importance. Only the democracies admitted that they suffered from internal class problems. (p. 831)

The dictatorships talked of the struggle between rich nations and poor nations, the "have" and "have not" countries. They transformed the problem of poverty into an international struggle and gave the impression that war might be a solution for social ills. (p. 831)

Anti-Semitism was inflamed by propagandists who wished people to feel their supposed racial purity more keenly or to forget the deeper problems of society, including poverty, unemployment, and economic inequities. (p. 830)

In the Nazi and Fascist ethics, war was a noble thing, and the love of peace a sign of decadence. Although Soviet theory regarded war with non-Soviet powers as inevitable someday, the Soviet regime did not preach war as a positive moral good. (p. 833)

XX.
THE
SECOND
WORLD WAR
SECTIONS 105–108, pp. 834–866

105. *The Weakness of the Democracies: Again to War*

Study Questions

1. What explanations may be suggested for the pacifism of the Western powers in the 1930s?
2. Describe the emergencies precipitated by Hitler from 1933 to the eve of the Munich crisis in September 1938. Of what special significance was the Rhineland episode?
3. Why was Italy dissatisfied with the peace arrangements of 1919?
4. How did the League of Nations respond (a) to Mussolini's invasion of Ethiopia, (b) to Japan's invasion of China?
5. How did the civil war in Spain affect international relations? public opinion in the United States and elsewhere? In what sense was the Spanish Civil War a rehearsal for the Second World War?
6. Why may the Munich crisis be considered the climax of the appeasement policy? Describe the position taken in the crisis by (a) the French, (b) the British, (c) the Russians.
7. Explain the circumstances under which the Western powers abandoned the policy of appeasement. Why did the negotiations with the Soviet Union fail?

Key Discussion Sentences

From the Japanese invasion of Manchuria in 1931 to the outbreak of European war in 1939, force was used by those who wished to revise the international order, but never by those who wished to maintain it.

The Spanish Civil War split the world into fascist and antifascist camps.

The Munich crisis revealed the helpless weakness into which the democracies had fallen.

The Nazi-Soviet Pact of August 1939 stupefied the world; it was recognized as the signal for war.

Identifications

Maginot Line	remilitarization of the	Marco Polo Bridge
Neville Chamberlain	Rhineland	Rome-Berlin Axis
U.S. neutrality	Haile Selassie	Anti-Comintern Pact
legislation	Spanish Popular Front	Sudeten Germans
Saar plebiscite	*Anschluss*	Munich conference
	Francisco Franco	Nazi-Soviet Pact
	nonintervention policy	

Map Exercise

1. Consult the map on pp. 728–729. Can you locate each of the trouble zones of the 1930s mentioned in Section 105?

106. The Years of Axis Triumph

Study Questions

1. Describe the opening stages of the Second World War in eastern Europe. Why was the opening stage of the war in the West called the "phony war"? How did this stage end?
2. What explanations have been given for the collapse of France? What happened to the country after defeat?
3. In what sense did Hitler dominate the European continent by the summer of 1940?
4. How did Britain react to the Nazi conquests? the United States? Explain the nature and results of the battle of Britain.
5. What explanations are there for Hitler's decision to invade Russia? Describe the results of his Russian campaign by the summer of 1942.
6. Describe major military developments in North Africa from 1940 to mid-1942.
7. What policies had the Japanese been following during the European war? What were the consequences of the Japanese attack in 1941?
8. Why may the autumn and winter of 1942 be called the blackest period of the war for the Soviet-Western alliance?

Key Discussion Sentences

In the winter of 1939–1940 all was deceptively quiet in the West.

The fall of France in June 1940 left the world aghast.

In 1940, as in 1807, only Great Britain remained at war with the conqueror of Europe.

In North Africa fortunes were fickle.

American opinion was divided over intervention in the war.

For the Soviet-Western alliance, 1942 was the year of dismay.

Identifications

blitzkrieg	Vidkun Quisling	El Alamein
Russo-Finnish War	genocide	General Tojo
Dunkirk	Four Freedoms	capture of Singapore
Vichy France	Lend-Lease	Greater East Asia Co-
Festung Europa	battle of Britain	Prosperity Sphere
"new order"	Ultra	Albert Speer
"scorched earth"	battle of Moscow	

Map Exercises

1. Study the map on pp. 850–851, "Europe, 1942." Which areas had been incorporated into Hitler's "empire"? Which states were allied with Germany in the war? occupied by the Axis? at war against the Axis? Consult also the map on p. 893, "Germany and Its Borders, 1919–1990" (middle panel).
2. Using the maps on pp. 850–851 and pp. 856–857, can you locate each of the places mentioned in Section 106?

107. The Western-Soviet Victory

Study Questions

1. Explain the nature of the combination aligned against the Axis by 1942. Why were the Russians dissatisfied with the failure to open a true "second front"?
2. What evidence was there in late 1942 and in 1943 that the tide was beginning to turn in favor of the Allies?
3. Describe the preparations for the invasion of Normandy, the nature of the military operation, and the events that followed. What setback did the Allies encounter in December 1944?
4. Describe the sweep of Russian operations in this same period. How did the war in Europe end?
5. What major operations had to be undertaken in the Pacific? How did the war end in that theater?
6. How would you compare military and civilian casualties in the Second World War with the casualties of the First?
7. What is meant by the Holocaust?
8. What is the painting by Grosz (p. 861) intended to communicate?

Key Discussion Sentences

By 1942 the alliance against the Axis aggressors that could not be created in the 1930s had at last been consummated.

From 1942 on, the Russians were suspicious of their Western allies.

The invasion of Europe was of a wholly unprecedented kind.

By the end of the war, the Russians were in control of the major capitals of central and eastern Europe.

While plans were being made for an invasion of Japan, two atomic bombs in August 1945 hastened the end of the war.

Identifications

Combined Chiefs of Staff	Admiral Darlan	battle of the "bulge"
Coral Sea and Midway	invasion of Sicily	Dresden
battle of the Atlantic	Marshal Badoglio	rising of the Polish underground
Stalingrad	Normandy	Katyn Forest massacre
invasion of North Africa	Resistance	Remagen
Okinawa	plot of July 20, 1944	genocide
	"Final Solution"	Auschwitz
	Admiral Doenitz	Leyte Gulf
	Hiroshima	

Map Exercises

1. Study the map on pp. 856–857. Explain the position of the Axis partners at the point of their maximum advances in 1942. What overall global threat seemed within the realm of possibility? What major phases of the war are shown for the Atlantic theater? the Pacific theater?
2. Study the map on p. 858, "The Holocaust." What does it tell you about the Nazi destruction of European Jewry?
3. Can you locate each of the places mentioned in Section 107?

108. The Foundations of the Peace

Study Questions

1. Discuss the "ideological basis" of the peace as it took form during the war.
2. What can be said for and against the demand for "unconditional surrender"?
3. What different attitudes toward the postwar settlement can be discerned in Roosevelt, Churchill, and Stalin respectively? What position did each of the wartime leaders take at (a) the Teheran conference, (b) the Yalta conference?
4. Of what significance were the circumstances under which the Yalta conference

took place? What major political decisions were reached at Yalta? What role did the war in the Far East play in these discussions? Evaluate the criticisms later made of these decisions.

5. Explain the agreements reached at Potsdam. Of what significance were the decisions made on the German eastern boundaries?
6. How did the peace settlement after the Second World War differ from the peace settlement after the First World War?

Key Discussion Sentences

In the Atlantic Charter, and in other wartime statements, the ideological basis of the peace was formulated and proclaimed.

Churchill, steeped in traditional balance-of-power politics, saw the need for bargaining and for making political arrangements in advance of the peace.

The strategy that would win the war in the next eighteen months, decided upon at Teheran, all but guaranteed Russian domination of eastern Europe.

Roosevelt was unwilling to disturb the unity of the Soviet-Western coalition in the global struggle.

At Yalta, Roosevelt and Churchill extracted from Stalin a number of promises for the areas he controlled, but the promises provided a false sense of agreement.

The Yalta agreement lent an aura of respectability to Soviet expansion.

It is doubtful whether the decision to demand "unconditional surrender" had any bearing on the outcome of events.

Identifications

Atlantic Charter	Curzon line	Kaliningrad
Casablanca conference	Morgenthau plan	Szczecin
Teheran conference	Potsdam conference	Declaration on Liber-
Yalta conference	Oder-Neisse boundary	ated Europe
United Nations	East Prussia	

Map Exercises

1. On the outline map of Europe, indicate the new political boundaries of eastern Europe at the end of the Second World War. Show (a) Russian territorial expansion in eastern Europe and (b) changes in the Polish-German border. Suggested source: *A History of the Modern World,* pp. 248, 758–759, and 893 (lower panel).
2. Which of the new Russian areas had been lost in the First World War? (See maps, pp. 562–563, 758–759.)

3. Explain: "Poland extended its territorial boundaries about a hundred miles westward as compensation for Russian westward expansion at Polish expense." (P. 865, and see maps, pp. 248, 758–759, and 893, top and bottom panels.)

GENERAL ESSAY QUESTIONS FOR CHAPTER XX

1. How would you compare the origins of the Second World War with the origins of the First? How was the coming of war in 1939 linked to dissatisfaction with the peace treaties of 1919? What special role did Adolf Hitler play in the coming of the Second World War?
2. Describe the successes of the Axis powers in the early years of the war. What were the stages in the eventual Western-Soviet victory? What factors contributed to that victory?
3. The Second World War has been called the greatest conflict in human history, in part because of the heavy toll of civilian lives. How would you assess the responsibility of each of the major powers for the destruction of civilian populations and for other atrocities during the war?
4. Why was the Soviet-Western wartime coalition unable to lay the foundations for the postwar world?

GENERAL DISCUSSION PASSAGES FOR CHAPTER XX

Peace in the abstract, the peace that is the mere absence of war, does not exist in international relations. Peace is never found apart from certain conditions. (p. 834)

The Nazi-Soviet Pact of August 23, 1939, stupefied the world. Communism and Nazism, supposed to be ideological opposites, had come together. A generation more versed in ideology than in power politics was dumbfounded. (pp. 842–843)

The Allies were fighting for a world, Roosevelt said, in which the Four Freedoms were to be secure—freedom of speech, freedom of worship, freedom from want, and freedom from fear. (p. 846)

Few realized, wrote General George C. Marshall some years later, how "close to complete domination of the world" were Germany and Japan in 1942, and "how thin the thread of Allied survival had been stretched." (p. 849)

Because precision bombardment of military targets proved difficult, the Allied air assaults became area bombings, and civilians were the largest casualties. (p. 853)

Stalingrad was a turning point not only in the history of the war but in the history of central and eastern Europe as well. (p. 854)

The Allied contribution to the Soviet war effort was indispensable, but Russian human losses were tremendous. The Russians lost more men in the battle of Stalingrad than the United States lost in combat during the entire war, in all theaters combined. (p. 854)

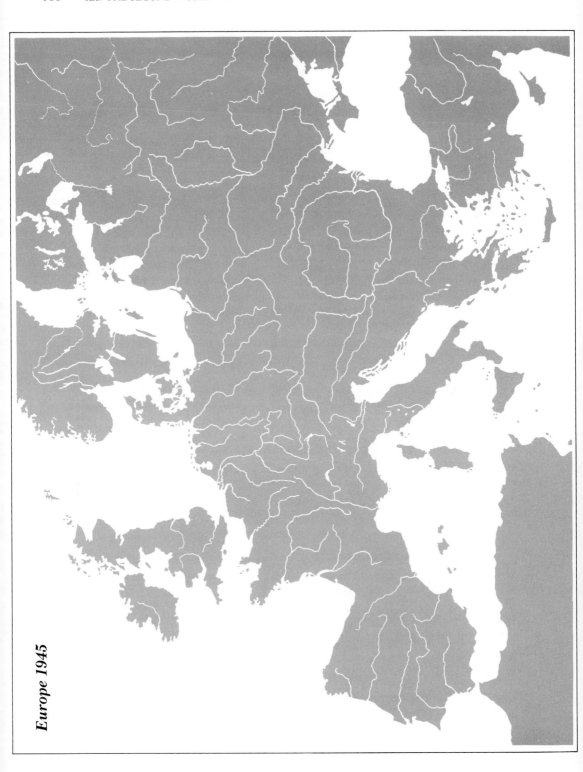

Europe 1945

Although word of the Nazi annihilation policy reached the outside world through the Vatican and other sources, the Allied leaders at first disbelieved the reports, and then, giving priority to their military objectives, did nothing to stop the systematic slaughter. (p. 858)

A generation reared to mistrust the fabricated atrocity tales of the First World War painfully, and belatedly, became aware of the real German horrors of the Second. Genocide, the effort to destroy a whole people, was the greatest of the Nazi sins against humanity. (p. 859)

The Second World War was the greatest conflict in human history. (p. 860)

Churchill, less sanguine of the future and of "diplomacy by friendship" than Roosevelt, would have preferred a franker recognition and definition of spheres of influence. But such ideas were ruled out as the thinking of a bygone era. (p. 865)

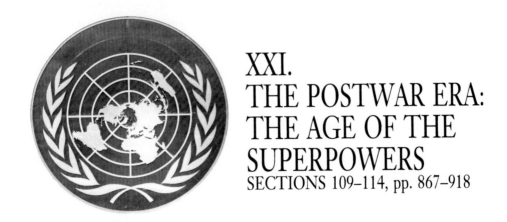

XXI.
THE POSTWAR ERA:
THE AGE OF THE
SUPERPOWERS
SECTIONS 109–114, pp. 867–918

109. The Cold War: The Opening Decade, 1945–1955

Study Questions

1. What motives may be suggested for Soviet conduct in the early postwar years? How did Soviet actions (a) in Europe, (b) elsewhere contribute to the Cold War?
2. How did President Truman and his advisers view Soviet actions in the early postwar years? What policies did the United States evolve?
3. Describe the circumstances and events that led to (a) the Truman Doctrine, (b) the Berlin airlift.
4. What unresolved questions are there about the origins of the Korean War? How did the United States perceive and react to the invasion? With what consequences and outcome?
5. Summarize the major episodes of the first Cold War decade. What was the status of the Cold War in 1955 (a) in Europe, (b) elsewhere?

Key Discussion Sentences

A diplomatic and ideological clash of interests emerged between the two superpowers that came to be known as the Cold War.

That the war left only two Great Powers standing in any strength created difficulties for international relations.

It was difficult for the West to distinguish between legitimate Soviet security needs and Soviet expansionism.

Soviet actions fed the belief that Stalin's ambitions transcended Eastern Europe.

The United States moved to fill the vacuum in the Mediterranean.

The Truman Doctrine committed the United States to unprecedented global responsibilities.

The Truman Doctrine, the Marshall Plan, and the Atlantic alliance were the three prongs of the American and Western response to the Soviet bid for global supremacy.

The rivalry over Europe ended in stalemate.

By 1950 the situation in East Asia had altered dramatically.

Korea, like Berlin, became another test of American and Western will.

Identifications

United Nations	Universal Declaration	Comecon
Great Power veto	of Human Rights	Warsaw Pact
Baruch Plan	Truman Doctrine	Japanese constitution
Cold War	Berlin blockade	Kim Il Sung
"containment"	Cominform	Yalu River
"iron curtain"	NATO	Korean War

Map Exercises

1. Study the map, pp. 872–873. How are the two stages of deportation and resettlement described? What were the major consequences by 1950?
2. By studying the maps of Contemporary Europe, front end papers, and Contemporary Asia, back end papers, can you locate each of the countries and areas that played a key role in the first decade of the Cold War?
3. Study the map, p. 679, "Northeast China and Adjoining Regions," and the map of Contemporary Asia, back end papers. (a) Why has this area historically been "one of the world's trouble zones"? (b) Can you locate the places mentioned in the discussion of the Korean War?

110. Western Europe: Economic Reconstruction

Study Questions

1. What motives may be suggested for the Marshall Plan? What did it accomplish?
2. Discuss the nature of the economies that emerged in Western Europe in the postwar years. How would you assess the record of economic growth in the years that followed?
3. How did the West European states meet social objectives as well as economic needs in these years?

Key Discussion Sentences

The results of the Marshall Plan exceeded the boldest anticipations of its American sponsors.

The United States used its economic resources to help revive its competitors, but the Marshall Plan also served American interests.

In all Western Europe economic growth became a central objective—virtually an obsession.

The prosperity of Western Europe derived from a competitive free market and private enterprise but was accompanied everywhere by an extensive role for government.

The postwar governments gave a high priority to social objectives.

Identifications

European Recovery
  Program
OEEC
"mixed economies"
Keynes

"countercyclical mea-
  sures"
"fine tuning"
Wirtschaftswunder
"thirty glorious years"

"guest workers"
welfare state

111. Western Europe: Political Reconstruction

Study Questions

1. What political problems did Western Europe face in the early postwar years? How were they met?
2. Describe the European political atmosphere in the early postwar years. How did it seem to change?
3. In what directions did the Labour party government set the course of British politics? What accounted for the shifting electoral fortunes of the two major parties in the next several decades?
4. Assess the accomplishments and shortcomings of the French Fourth Republic.
5. How did the French Fifth Republic come into existence? Describe the new constitutional arrangements. How did they work out? What role did de Gaulle play in the origins and history of the new republic?
6. How was the constitutional and political machinery of the Federal Republic of Germany designed to overcome problems of the past? How successfully did it operate? What role did Adenauer play?
7. What paradox did the Italian Republic seem to present? What role did the Christian Democratic party play in Italian political life? the Italian Communist party?

Key Discussion Sentences

A renovating spirit swept Western Europe in the early postwar years.

Christian Democratic parties played a key role in shaping the new regimes in Western Europe.

In 1945 Britain became the world's chief exemplar of parliamentary socialism and the modern welfare state.

Until the late 1970s the question was whether Labour or the Conservatives could better manage British decline.

The French Fourth Republic in its machinery of government differed in only a few details from the Third.

The presidency became the fulcrum of power in the French Fifth Republic.

De Gaulle settled the Algerian crisis in his own way.

The founders of the Federal Republic of Germany deliberately set out to avoid the weaknesses of the Weimar Republic.

Adenauer successfully integrated the Federal Republic of Germany into the political, economic, and military structures of Western Europe.

The unstable political scene in the Italian Republic did not interfere with unprecedented economic growth and prosperity.

Identifications

Beveridge Report
Clement Attlee
MRP
Pierre Mendès-France
Monnet Plan
Charles de Gaulle

Nuremberg trials
Konrad Adenauer
Christian Democrats
Social Democrats
"social market
  economy"
"Basic Law"
codetermination law

Willy Brandt
Free Democrats
Ostpolitik
Alcide De Gasperi
Eurocommunism

Map Exercise

1. Study the map, p. 893, "Germany and Its Borders, 1919–1990," upper and lower panels. Can you locate the "two Germanys"? How do the German eastern borders in 1945 differ from those in 1919? What happened to East Prussia? (See pp. 864–865, map, pp. 728–729, and front end papers.)

112. Reshaping the Global Economy

Study Questions

1. What wartime steps did the United States and Britain take to shape the postwar world economy?
2. What was meant by the "world economy" in the postwar years? How successfully was world trade liberalized?

3. How would you assess the efforts taken to stabilize world currencies? How has the world's monetary system evolved since 1971?
4. What path did West European integration take? Discuss the origins, nature, and accomplishments of the European Economic Community. How did it evolve into the European Community?
5. What changes from the 1960s on challenged America's economic leadership?

Key Discussion Sentences

Wartime planners developed a bold initiative to reshape the postwar world economy.

Trade agreements contributed to the vast expansion of world trade.

Currency stabilization turned out to be more difficult than anticipated.

As Western Europe expanded economically, it also drew closer together.

The European Economic Community, in operation in 1958, became one of the world's thriving economic aggregates.

The more dedicated Europeanists remained disappointed.

The world continued to grope its way toward new monetary arrangements.

Identifications

Bretton Woods	Council of Europe	European Community
"most favored nation"	European Coal and	European Parliament
GATT	Steel Community	"Eurodollars"
International Monetary	Treaty of Rome	gold-dollar standard
Fund	Common Market	European Monetary
Jean Monnet		System

113. The Communist World: The U.S.S.R. and Eastern Europe

Study Questions

1. Describe the U.S.S.R. in the last years of Stalin's rule. What may be said about the Stalin era as a whole?
2. What were the accomplishments and shortcomings of the Soviet centrally planned economy?
3. Discuss the nature and results of Khrushchev's efforts at reform. What led to his downfall?
4. How would you characterize the Brezhnev era in such areas as (a) military defense, (b) the economy, (c) Soviet society, (d) foreign affairs?
5. How did the Soviets come to dominate Eastern Europe? How did they

consolidate their control in the early postwar years? What economic changes took place in the East European countries?

6. Discuss the restlessness in the Soviet satellites in the 1950s and 1960s. How did the Soviets react (a) in Poland, (b) in Hungary, (c) in Czechoslovakia?

7. Discuss the growing integration of Eastern Europe into the world economy in the 1960s.

Key Discussion Sentences

Stalin had a massive impact during his close to thirty years in power.

Khrushchev was shrewd enough to recognize the need for change, but there were clear limits to the reforms the party and bureaucracy would tolerate.

The superficial stability of the Brezhnev years concealed social tensions and economic failures.

The Soviet Union ranked as a formidable military and nuclear superpower but not as a modern industrial society.

By the 1960s, despite political repression, a rural, agrarian Eastern Europe was being shaped into an urban, industrial society.

The Soviets in the 1950s and 1960s made clear the limits to which they would tolerate freedom and independence in central and eastern Europe.

Identifications

"doctors' plot"	dissidents	Tito
Lavrenti Beria	*apparatchki*	Gomulka
de-Stalinization	*nomenklatura*	Imre Nagy
"crimes of the Stalin era"	*samizdat*	János Kádár
the "thaw"	Sakharov	"goulash communism"
Boris Pasternak	Andropov	Alexander Dubcek
Solzhenitsyn	Chernenko	"Prague spring"
	KGB	Brezhnev Doctrine

Map Exercises

1. By examining the maps on p. 1034 and the front end papers, can you locate the areas of central and eastern Europe that fell into the Soviet sphere of influence after the Second World War? What happened to the Baltic republics? Finland? (See pp. 909–911.)

2. In what sense could the "iron curtain" be said to have descended roughly along the old "Elbe-Trieste line"? Why has that line been called "one of the most important sociological boundaries in the history of modern Europe"? (See map and caption, pp. 212–213.)

114. The Communist World: The People's Republic of China

Study Questions

1. How did the Communist regime under Mao transform China?
2. What may be said about Mao's more radical attempts at social engineering?
3. Discuss China's relations during these years (a) with the U.S.S.R., (b) with the West.
4. How would you assess Mao's place in Chinese history?

Key Discussion Sentences

The Chinese leaned heavily on Soviet experience.

The new regime mobilized the nation to rebuild the war-devastated economy and to transform the country into an industrial power.

The regime transformed life in many ways.

The Great Leap Forward turned into a disaster.

In 1966 and for several years thereafter the country was convulsed by the Cultural Revolution.

Although professing peace, China pursued an aggressive foreign policy.

The emergence of China as a second major Communist power undermined the ideological leadership of the Soviet Union.

Mao's successors praised him for his monumental achievements but criticized him for his "grave blunders."

Identifications

Kuomintang	"rightists"	Red Guards
Republic of China (Taiwan)	"Great Leap Forward"	Zhou En-lai
People's Republic of China	Cultural Revolution	*The Living Thoughts of Chairman Mao*
	Tibet	Great Helmsman
	Pinyin	

GENERAL ESSAY QUESTIONS FOR CHAPTER XXI

1. Explain the origins of the Cold War. How did perceptions and misperceptions on both sides contribute to it? What form did it take in the first postwar decade?
2. What was meant by the policy of "containment"? What did it accomplish in the years 1945–1955?

3. Discuss the emergence in the postwar era of (a) the political systems, (b) the economies of the major West European nations.
4. How did wartime planning help reshape the postwar global economy? What role did (a) the United States, (b) Western Europe, (c) Japan play in the postwar economy?
5. What forms did the movement for European unification take in the postwar era?
6. How did the Soviets react to the restlessness in the East European satellite states? What impact did the Soviet actions have on international communism? How did the People's Republic of China pose a challenge to Soviet ideological leadership?

GENERAL DISCUSSION PASSAGES FOR CHAPTER XXI

The world has been in the grip of a cataclysm since 1914. (p. 867)

Certain problems that have confronted mankind for over a century became even more complex and more urgent in the second half of the century. Three can be singled out: science, the organization of industrial society, and national sovereignty. (p. 868)

That science had provided the means to annihilate civilization was especially shocking to a world that had set one of its highest values on scientific progress. (p. 868)

Americans expended a good deal more effort trying to correct the lack of security in their system than the Soviets did to correct the lack of freedom. (p. 868)

It was difficult to distinguish between what might have been legitimate security needs of the Soviets and expansionist missionary zeal. (p. 871)

In time, Americans, too, became obsessed with a missionary zeal of their own. (p. 871)

Anticommunism in Asia and elsewhere did not necessarily equate with democratic government. (p. 879)

The Truman Doctrine committed the United States to unprecedented global responsibilities. (p. 874)

The prosperity of Western Europe derived from a competitive free market and a private enterprise economy but was accompanied everywhere by extensive economic planning, systematic government intervention, and a network of social services. (p. 885)

The presence of new Europeans led to friction, often overtly racial, testing the flexibility and tolerance of a European society becoming increasingly multiethnic and multicultural. (p. 886)

The European Community helped end the internecine rivalries that had exhausted the continent in the first half of the twentieth century. (pp. 900–901)

The European Community created a strong sense of common destiny, shared faith in democratic institutions and market economies, and a concern for human rights and social needs. (p. 902)

At the Nuremberg trials of the Nazi leaders the evidence of evil deeds was set down for posterity in many volumes of testimony. Although misgivings arose about the trials, they contributed in their way to reinforcing international standards of civilized behavior. (p. 892)

The Bolshevik Revolution, in the loss of human lives, must be counted among the costliest experiments in social engineering in all history. (p. 904)

In later years, in a freer atmosphere, the question was debated whether Stalin's dictatorship represented a logical outcome of the Bolshevik Revolution or was an aberration. (p. 904)

More profoundly than the Russian, the Chinese Revolution refashioned the habits and ethos of a gigantic population, reaching remote villages and hamlets untouched for centuries. (p. 916)

Mao's teachings on imperialism and on the vanguard role of the peasantry, and his successes in guerrilla warfare, influenced revolutionaries all over the world. (p. 917)

XXII.
EMPIRES INTO NATIONS: THE DEVELOPING WORLD
SECTIONS 115–119, pp. 919–963
PICTURE ESSAY, pp. 965–977

115. *End of the European Empires in Asia*

Study Questions

1. How did the Second World War contribute to the undermining of the European colonial empires? What role did the nationalist movements play? How did the European countries react?
2. Describe the background to the struggle for independence in India and its outcome. How was the religious issue met?
3. What did Nehru's leadership in India accomplish in the early years of independence? What problems persisted?
4. Describe the course of events in Pakistan after independence. What circumstances led to the secession of Bangladesh? With what consequences?
5. Describe Indonesia's experience (a) in the struggle for independence, (b) in the years after independence.
6. What justification did France advance for its war in Indochina? What relationship was there in Asia between nationalism and communism? Why?

Key Discussion Sentences

Wartime ideology reinforced nationalist agitation for independence and freedom.

Within two decades after 1945 the major European colonial empires disappeared, some without a struggle, others after protracted wars.

The end in 1947 of British rule in India was epoch-making.

In the postcolonial era India's political experience was unique.

The French colonial empire in Indochina fell apart, but not without a struggle.

Communism in Asia was often linked to nationalism, anticolonialism, anti-Westernism, and genuine popular discontent.

In many parts of postcolonial Asia there was often no absolute repression but no genuine democracy either.

Identifications

"Third World"	Bangladesh	Dien Bien Phu
"quit India"	Sri Lanka	Ho Chi Minh
Congress party	Commonwealth	Indira Gandhi
Muslim League	Sukarno	Benazir Bhutto
Jawaharlal Nehru	Suharto	Myanmar
Bandung Conference	"guided democracy"	Corazón Aquino
Jinnah		

Map Exercise

1. Using the maps, "The World about 1970," pp. 980–981, and "Contemporary Asia," back end papers, can you locate each of the states in Asia that gained independence in the postwar years?

116. The African Revolution

Study Questions

1. Why did the French resist the Algerian struggle for independence? What repercussions did the French-Algerian War have on France itself? What has been the history of Algeria since independence?
2. How did the French colonial empire in sub-Saharan Africa end?
3. How did the British respond to nationalist pressures (a) in West Africa, (b) in East Africa? What course did developments take in southern Africa?
4. Describe the course of events in South Africa from 1948 to the present. How was apartheid overcome?
5. What special events accompanied independence in the Belgian Congo? What has been the subsequent history of Zaire?
6. How did Portugal react to the pressures from its colonies for independence? With what consequences for Portugal itself? What has been the subsequent history of the former Portuguese colonies?
7. Why is it possible to speak of an "African Revolution"? What general observations may be made about the new African nations in the decades of independence?

Key Discussion Sentences

For Africa one age came to a close after the Second World War and a new era opened.

The new African states differed from the older European nations in many ways.

For a time the Nigerian federal republic offered a democratic model for the rest of the continent.

The catalogue of disaster and suffering in Africa in the first generation of independence was grim.

Independence provided a deep source of self-esteem for the new African nations.

The unfinished item on the political agenda of the African Revolution long remained the extension of democratic rights to the black majority in South Africa.

The African Revolution brought an end to Western colonialism but did not bring with it democratic government or civil and human rights.

Identifications

Kwame Nkrumah
"African socialism"
Biafra
Jomo Kenyatta
Julius Nyerere
Milton Obote
Idi Amin
Afrikaans

Zimbabwe
Afrikaner
Nationalist party
apartheid
Nelson Mandela
"bantustan"
de Klerk
Namibia
African National
  Congress

francophone Africa
Patrice Lumumba
Mobutu
Horn of Africa
uhuru
négritude
Liberia
Burundi
Rwanda

Map Exercises

1. "Only a map of contemporary Africa can communicate the vast political transformation that had occurred" (p. 937). How does a comparison of the maps on pp. 667 and 927 communicate this "vast political transformation"? What do the maps on pp. 665 and 667 tell you about precolonial Africa? about Africa in 1914?
2. Can you locate each of the countries in Africa mentioned in this section?
3. Using the outline map, sketch the approximate boundaries of the larger African states. Suggested source: *A History of the Modern World*, p. 927.

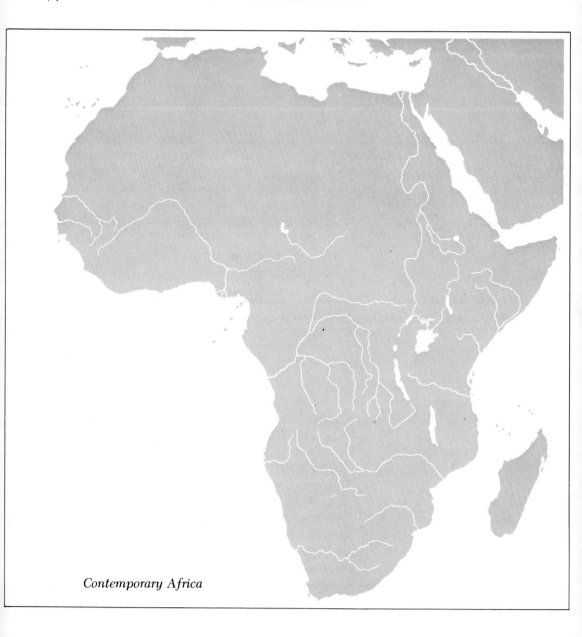

Contemporary Africa

117. *Ferment in the Middle East*

Study Questions

1. What general observations may be made about modernization in the Islamic world?
2. Which are the principal non-Arab Muslim states? How did the Arab states acquire independence? What may be said about pan-Arabism in the post-1945 world?
3. How did (a) Zionism, (b) events during the Second World War, and (c) the British mandate over Palestine contribute to the creation of the new state of Israel? What kind of government, economy, and society emerged?
4. Summarize the causes and outcome of the Arab-Israeli wars in the years 1948–1982. Why were Arab-Israeli tensions difficult to resolve? Of what significance was the agreement signed in 1993?
5. Describe (a) the origins and nature of the revolution in Iran, (b) United States relationships with Iran before and after the revolution.
6. Discuss the origins, nature, and outcome of the Iran-Iraq War. Why did it lead to international intervention?
7. Describe the crisis resulting from Iraq's invasion of Kuwait in 1990. What role did the United States play? What were the results of the international intervention?

Key Discussion Sentences

The Islamic world was determined to share in Western material advances on its own terms.

Pan-Arabism failed to rally much support.

Israel in the decades after independence built a Western-style, urban, industrial, and democratic society.

From the beginning the Arab states viewed Israel as a Western-backed intrusion into their lands.

Arab-Israeli tensions brought wider international forces into play and made the Middle East one of the most turbulent parts of the world.

The revolutionary events in Iran unsettled the Islamic world as well as the West.

To protect the flow of oil through the Persian Gulf the industrial countries resorted to force.

The American and allied forces compelled Iraq to withdraw from Kuwait but failed to dislodge the dictator from power.

Identifications

Balfour declaration	Lebanon	Ayotollah Khomeini
Arab League	pan-Arabism	*chador*
jehad	Hafez al-Assad	Saddam Hussein
Nasser	*intifada*	Arab Baath Socialist
Anwar al-Sadat	Mossadegh	Party
Yasir Arafat	Muhammad Reza	Iran-Iraq War
Qaddafi	Shiite	Persian Gulf War
PLO	Sunni	

Map Exercises

1. Study the map on p. 941. What does it tell you of the Arab world? How would you identify the larger Islamic world? (See also p. 940 and map, "Contemporary Asia," back end papers.)
2. Study the map on p. 945. What do the five panels tell you about the emergence of Israel and the changes in its territorial boundaries since independence? What is meant by the "occupied territories"? the West Bank? the Gaza Strip?
3. Study the map on p. 950. What does it tell you about the flow of oil from the Middle East? the importance of the Persian Gulf? Can you locate the places and areas mentioned in the account of (a) the Iran-Iraq war of 1980–1988, (b) the Persian Gulf War of 1990–1991?

118. *Changing Latin America*

Study Questions

1. What did the legacy of (a) colonialism, (b) the wars for independence mean for Latin America?
2. What role did British and American economic interests play in the development of Latin America?
3. How was the region affected by (a) the years of dependence on the outside world, (b) the depression years, (c) the Second World War? Discuss the record of economic development since 1945.
4. Discuss the relationship with the United States (a) in the nineteenth century, (b) in the first half of the twentieth century, (c) in the years since the Second World War.
5. What general observations may be made about the political record of Latin America in the twentieth century? What examples can you cite to reinforce these statements?
6. Discuss the nature and results of social revolution (a) in the Mexican Revolution, (b) in Cuba under Fidel Castro.
7. What continuing political, economic, and social problems does Latin America face? How would you differentiate among the various countries of the region?

Key Discussion Sentences

The legacy of colonialism left Latin America economically dependent on the outside world.

The Latin American political record in the twentieth century reflected a basic instability.

Military regimes promoted industrialization but tended to neglect social issues.

Several of the Latin American countries could be ranked among the newly industrialized countries of the world; others were among the most depressed.

The most sweeping attempt at social revolution occurred in Cuba.

Latin America still faced deep-seated social problems, many of them the legacy of its history.

Identifications

mestizo	Getulio Vargas	Salvador Allende
caudillo	Institutional Revolution-	*fidelismo*
"dollar diplomacy"	ary party	Augusto Pinochet
Lázaro Cárdenas	OAS	North American Free
"good neighbor" policy	"liberation theology"	Trade Agreement
"import substitution"	the "disappeared"	Shining Path
peronismo		

Map Exercises

1. What is meant by Latin America? (See p. 952.)
2. Using the outline map, sketch the approximate boundaries of the larger Latin American states. Suggested source: *A History of the Modern World*, p. 980.

119. *The Developing World*

PICTURE ESSAY: THE MODERN WORLD IN VARIED SETTINGS
(pp. 965–977)

Study Questions

1. What were the expectations for the developing world after the Second World War?
2. Describe (a) the models of development that were available, (b) the advantages and disadvantages of each.
3. Explain the record of development in the 1960s and the subsequent experience. What conclusions may be drawn from the table on p. 961?

The Western Hemisphere

4. Discuss the major grievances expressed by the developing countries. What changes in the international economy did they propose?
5. How would you assess the development experience as a whole?
6. Explain the various ways in which the Picture Essay demonstrates the emergence of "modernity" in different cultural contexts. What does it suggest about the blending of modern and traditional values in the contemporary world? Can you cite additional examples?

Key Discussion Sentences

The countries not part of the industrial world looked forward to modernization, economic growth, and social progress.

In the 1960s it was possible to speak of "a revolution of rising expectations."

The Third World countries argued for a reshaping of the international economy.

Four decades of the development experience showed mixed results.

The developing countries were far from homogeneous.

In the 1980s economic growth in the Third World even regressed.

Many of the developing countries left the Third World behind.

Identifications

"development decade"	"north-south" contest	"Fourth World"
Green Revolution	Pacific Rim	NIC
"New International Economic Order"	"little tigers"	"purchasing power parity"

Map Exercise

1. Study the maps on pp. 980–981 and the front and back end papers. In what sense did the tensions between the developing and the industrial world take on the configuration of a "north-south" contest (p. 961)?

GENERAL ESSAY QUESTIONS FOR CHAPTER XXII

1. How would you assess the legacy of Western imperialism? What positive and negative aspects need to be stressed?
2. What accounted for the spectacular end of the European colonial empires after the Second World War? In what ways did the European nations react to the agitation for independence?
3. What may be said about the experiences of the newly independent nations in Asia and Africa in the decades after independence (a) from a political viewpoint, (b) from an economic viewpoint?
4. Summarize the political and economic experience of the Latin American

nations in the years since 1945. How successful were they in overcoming the
legacy of their past?

5. In what sense did the Middle East become one of the world's most troubled
   areas in the contemporary era?

GENERAL DISCUSSION PASSAGES FOR CHAPTER XXII

Of all the great political changes in the history of the modern world, nothing was
more revolutionary, more dramatic, or more unexpected than the end of the
European overseas colonial empires. (p. 919)

The end of the colonial empires and the emergence of the new nations must
count among the most far-reaching consequences of the two World Wars, and
especially of the Second. (p. 920)

In Africa (and in Asia) the charismatic nationalist leaders often turned into
personal dictators once independence was won. (p. 929)

The African Revolution brought an end to Western colonialism and ushered in a
new era of independence, national sovereignty, and self-esteem but did not bring
with it democratic government, civil and human rights, the resolution of ethnic
and regional antagonisms, or a meaningful improvement in the quality of human
life. (p. 938)

The Iranian Revolution raised the larger question whether traditional Islamic
values, rigidly enforced, could accommodate secularism, modernization, democracy, and a pluralist society. (p. 951)

The age of imperialism left a permanent scar on subject peoples all over the
globe. Yet it was also the instrument whereby many of the scientific, material,
intellectual, and humanitarian achievements of the West spread to other parts of
the globe. (p. 959)

Although its political meaning has been eroded by the collapse of Soviet
communism, the term "Third World" in its economic sense seems destined to
survive. (p. 920)

In point of fact, there was no Third World. There were only two worlds, one
relatively rich, one poor. (p. 963)

An estimated 1.2 billion human beings, almost one-fourth the world's population,
lived in absolute poverty, in sub-Saharan Africa, Asia, Latin America, and the
Middle East. (p. 962)

The Latin American nations, despite their more than a century of political
independence by 1945, shared in many of the same experiences as the developing
nations of Asia and Africa. (p. 920)

Some Latin American leaders contended that social problems would be resolved
by economic progress and that excessive investment in social welfare might even
impede economic growth. (p. 956)

The United States, which had its own history of racial oppression and had gone through its own civil rights revolution, joined with others in pressing South Africa to end apartheid. (p. 933)

The countries with the most success in economic growth moved forward within the framework of market economies, but the debate continued over the role of government in stimulating development. (p. 962)

There is a new global uniformity in certain aspects of civilization, which is not a matter of Westernization or of Americanization. (p. 965)

XXIII.
A WORLD
ENDANGERED:
THE COLD WAR
SECTIONS 120–123, pp. 978–1010

120. Confrontation and Détente, 1955–1975

Study Questions

1. What observations may be made about Soviet-American relations in the years 1955 to 1964? What policies did Khrushchev follow?
2. How did President Kennedy respond to the Cuban missile crisis? How did it end?
3. Explain the origins of the Vietnam War and describe the stages of American involvement. How did President Johnson view the war? Why was the war so divisive in American political life?
4. How did President Nixon and Henry Kissinger analyze the international scene? With what results for American foreign policy?
5. Of what significance was the Helsinki conference of 1975?

Key Discussion Sentences

In the years after 1955 U.S.-Soviet relations seesawed between conciliation and crisis.

In the 1960s the nuclear arms race escalated.

The Berlin Wall built in 1961 stood as a grim physical reminder of the Cold War.

The gravest direct Soviet-American confrontation came over the Cuban missile crisis.

The debate went on as to whether the Vietnam War was part of the global struggle between communism and democracy or a civil war.

For the United States the Vietnam War was a searing experience.

De Gaulle rejected the rigid patterns of the Cold War.

The Nixon-Kissinger policies grew out of a reassessment of global realities.

Ancient rivalries prolonged the agonies of Southeast Asia. There was no monolithic communism in this part of the globe.

Helsinki was the high point of the era of détente.

Identifications

"peaceful coexistence"	Berlin Wall	Tet offensive
"spirit of Camp David"	Ho Chi Minh	Brezhnev Doctrine
Eisenhower Doctrine	Geneva Conference of	SALT I Treaty
flexible response	1954	détente
ICBM	Gulf of Tonkin	Helsinki accords
Bay of Pigs	resolution	

Map Exercises

1. Study the map on p. 986. Indicate the major developments that took place in Southeast Asia in the years 1946–1975. (See also pp. 924–925 and map, pp. 676–677.)
2. Study the map on pp. 980–981. What major changes may be noted in the world map since the end of the Second World War?

121. The Global Economy

Study Questions

1. Why did the Arab oil embargo of 1973–1974 have so serious an impact on the world economy? How did it affect Western Europe?
2. Explain the nature of the recession that began in 1974. How did it compare to the Great Depression of the 1930s? How did the economic situation confound Keynesian theory?
3. Discuss political changes from the mid-1970s to 1990 (a) in Britain, (b) in France, (c) in the Federal Republic of Germany, (d) elsewhere in Western Europe.
4. Discuss the continuing strengths and weaknesses of the American economy. What special problems did it face? What were the possible consequences?
5. Explain the debate over the contemporary welfare state. What views did Margaret Thatcher and Ronald Reagan seem to share?
6. Describe the expansion of the European Community after 1969. What new tensions arose? What key changes occurred in the early 1990s?
7. Explain the concerns about the future direction of international trade.

Key Discussion Sentences

The oil crisis and recession interrupted the spectacular growth of the West European economies.

Never had an essential commodity risen in price so rapidly; never did the whole Western industrial complex seem so vulnerable.

Faith in Keynesianism, and even in the welfare state, was shaken.

The return of prosperity in the 1980s reinforced confidence in the free-market economy despite the vicissitudes of the business cycle.

The impact of the Thatcher years in Britain was decisive.

When Socialists took office in Western Europe, modernization, economic growth, and market economies overshadowed, if they did not entirely replace, older ideologies.

Even with prosperity, the United States showed trade, balance-of-payments, and budget deficits.

Despite its problems, the United States was still the premier political, economic, and military power.

The European Community became the European Union.

The world's financial markets and currencies were more interdependent than ever before.

Identifications

OPEC	Margaret Thatcher	Helmut Kohl
"stagflation"	Falkland Islands	OECD
Keynesian theory	François Mitterrand	"common agricultural
welfare state	Bettino Craxi	policy"
"trickle down" theory	Felipe Gonzalez	a "single Europe"
	"postindustrial" age	Maastricht Treaty

122. *The Cold War Rekindled*

Study Questions

1. What form did the Cold War assume under the Carter presidency? How did President Carter react to the Soviet invasion of Afghanistan?
2. What approach did President Reagan take to the Cold War? What actions did he take in the Western Hemisphere? elsewhere?
3. Discuss the escalation of the nuclear arms race from the 1960s to the mid-

1980s. What was meant by the doctrine of "deterrence"? the "balance of terror"? What form did the debate take between proponents and critics of these policies? What position did President Reagan take?

Key Discussion Sentences

Under President Carter, détente with the Soviet Union was linked to respect for human rights, which he said must be "the soul of our foreign policy."

There was no doubt of President Reagan's commitment to a hard line in the Cold War.

Guided missiles became the key strategic weapons of the modern age.

Nuclear arms were built not for use but for deterrence.

In the rekindled Cold War of the early 1980s there seemed to be no solution to the arms impasse.

Identifications

SALT II treaty	MAD	"nuclear winter"
partial test-ban treaty	antiballistic missiles	Afghanistan
nonproliferation treaty	"hot line"	Grenada

123. China after Mao

Study Questions

1. Explain the nature and results of Deng's reform program. To what extent did he change the system inherited from Mao?
2. What serious flaws developed in the economic program?
3. What attitude did Deng and the party leaders take toward political reform and democratization? With what consequences?

Key Discussion Sentences

Deng spoke of "a marriage between a planned and market economy."

Ideology took a back seat to material advance.

What brought the memorable decade of reform to a close was the refusal to permit democratization.

By one measure China's economic output in the mid-1990s was ranked third in the world.

The pressure of expanding population made enormous demands on the economy.

Identifications

Deng Xiaoping
Jiang Qing
"iron rice bowl"

Hu Yaobang
Zhao Ziyang
"democracy
    movement"

Tiananmen Square
"mandate of Heaven"
"people's democratic
    dictatorship"

GENERAL ESSAY QUESTIONS FOR CHAPTER XXIII

1. How would you sketch the history of the Cold War during the years 1945–1975? Include (a) wartime origins, (b) the immediate postwar era, (c) the Krushchev and Brezhnev years. In what sense did relations seesaw between crisis and conciliation?
2. The United States fought two undeclared wars in the years 1945–1973. Discuss the origins, nature, and outcome of (a) the Korean War, (b) the Vietnam War. Why was the Vietnam War so much more divisive an experience?
3. Describe and discuss the nuclear arms competition in the years since 1945. What strategic doctrines evolved? What successes and what failures were there in arms limitation? Why is this chapter entitled "A World Endangered"?
4. What major challenges did the global economy face after 1974? the American economy? the European Community?
5. Discuss the reaction in the 1980s to the kind of welfare state that had emerged after the Second World War. How was the reaction manifested (a) in Britain, (b) in the United States, (c) elsewhere?
6. Describe the successive steps in the European unification movement from the 1950s to the mid-1990s. How would you evaluate the successes and failures of the movement?

GENERAL DISCUSSION PASSAGES FOR CHAPTER XXIII

American foreign policy in the Cold War remained firmly based on the premise that all unrest was Soviet-inspired. (p. 982)

The world entered a new era of military technology. Nuclear arms were built not for use but for deterrence. (p. 1004)

During the Cold War some questioned whether the United States, despite its enormous strength, should assume the responsibility, or even had the capability, to police the world against Communist aggression. (p. 988)

Interdependence is a form of dependency, and the expansion of the global economy after 1945 made each country vulnerable to events in distant places. (p. 992)

There was always the danger of a return to global protectionism. (p. 1001)

The welfare state was challenged as costly, wasteful, paternalistic, and bureaucratic, and as undermining individual responsibility and initiative. (p. 994)

The defenders of the welfare state argued that free-market economies had to be supplemented by government action to meet individual and social needs. (p. 995)

Some wondered whether the United States, still the premier economic and military power, might lose its primacy because of economic weaknesses—as Spain, France, and Britain had in the modern centuries. (p. 999)

Even if the more ambitious dream of a United States of Europe went unrealized, the European Union, for all its problems, remained an important and vibrant institution. (p. 1000)

The democracy movement in China demonstrated how deeply liberal values—or "bourgeois liberalism," as it was denounced—had penetrated China. (p. 1010)

XXIV.
A WORLD
TRANSFORMED
SECTIONS 124–129, pp. 1011–1065

124. The Crisis in the Soviet Union

Study Questions

1. How did centralized planning serve the U.S.S.R. in earlier years? Why did it seem unsuited for later needs?
2. Discuss the link in Gorbachev's program between economic reform and political liberalization.
3. What criticisms of Soviet society were openly voiced in the Gorbachev era?
4. Discuss Gorbachev's economic reforms. What did they fail to achieve? What criticisms were heard?
5. How did the relaxation of controls unleash ethnic unrest? What did this unrest reveal about the nature of the U.S.S.R.?
6. In what way was Gorbachev's foreign policy linked to his domestic program? How did this lead to a new kind of détente? to the end of the Cold War?

Key Discussion Sentences

Some of the basic structures of Soviet communism, developed since the Revolution, began to come apart in the 1980s.

For his economic reforms to succeed Gorbachev needed the support of the country, which he hoped to win through political change.

Even if *glasnost* had a more limited objective, it took on a dynamic of its own.

Gorbachev was bent on saving the Communist system by reforming it.

The country remained divided between an old guard that resisted reform and democratic reformers who believed that Gorbachev had not gone far enough.

Identifications

perestroika	Sakharov	intermediate range nuclear missile
glasnost	Congress of People's	
R.S.F.S.R.	Deputies	strategic arms treaty
Armenia-Azerbaijan dispute	Reagan-Gorbachev summits	

Map Exercise

1. Study the map of the U.S.S.R. on pp. 758–759, the population table on p. 754, and the table of nationalities on p. 1016. What do the two tables tell you about each of the constituent republics? What generalizations may be made about population changes since 1940? about ethnic pluralism in the former Soviet Union?

125. *The Revolutions of 1989 in Central and Eastern Europe*

Study Questions

1. How did central and eastern Europe change in the years of détente? What criticisms were heard in these countries about their centrally planned economies? their political systems? Of what importance were Gorbachev's reforms in the Soviet Union?
2. What role did Solidarity play in Poland? How did the Polish government react? What other forms of resistance to the regime emerged?
3. Describe the origins, course, and outcome of the revolutions of 1989 in (a) Poland, (b) Hungary, (c) the German Democratic Republic, (d) Czechoslovakia, (e) Romania, (f) Bulgaria.
4. What characteristics did the revolutions of 1989 in central and eastern Europe share? What problems did the new regimes face?
5. What international issues did the question of German reunification present? How were they met?

Key Discussion Sentences

Cracks and fissures had begun to appear in the satellite states in eastern Europe since the 1960s.

Gorbachev's example in the Soviet Union reinforced east European reform movements.

The masses of people demonstrating in central and eastern Europe voiced common grievances.

The dike in eastern Europe was first breached in Poland.

In 1989, as in 1848, a flood of revolutionary change swept in.

The ruling elites, without Soviet support, lost the will to govern under what was for them, too, an alien system.

The revolution, except in Romania, was carried out for the most part peacefully.

In Czechoslovakia it was said: "'89 is '68 upside down."

Once the German Democratic Republic was no longer a Communist state, pressure for reunification mounted.

With the revolutions of 1989 central and eastern Europe could rejoin the west.

Identifications

dissidents
Gomulka
Gierek
Lech Walesa
General Jaruzelski
Solidarity

János Kádár
Erich Honecker
Berlin Wall
Charter '77
"civil society"
"velvet revolution"

Civic Forum
Vaclav Havel
Ceausescu
the "German question"
Federal Republic of
    Germany

Map Exercises

1. Study the maps on p. 893 (upper and lower panels) and the front end papers. Describe the boundaries of reunified Germany. How do they differ from those of the interwar years?
2. Can you locate each of the places mentioned in Section 125?

126. The Collapse of Communism in the Soviet Union

Study Questions

1. How did the Gorbachev reforms contribute to the collapse of communism in the Soviet Union? Which reforms did the old guard most resent? What changes did the democratic reformers want? the constituent republics?
2. What did the democratic reformers mean by a "creeping coup d'état"?
3. Describe the emergent role of Boris N. Yeltsin. What new power base did he use?
4. Describe the events that led to the collapse of the Soviet Union. What role did Gorbachev play? Yeltsin?
5. Explain the nature and membership of the Commonwealth of Independent States. Which former Soviet republics became members? Which did not?

Key Discussion Sentences

Gorbachev vacillated between the reformers and hard-line conservatives.

For the old guard hard-liners the "union treaty" was the final straw.

The plotters turned out to be feckless and irresolute bunglers.

The collapse of the Communist regime was the culmination of the Gorbachev reform era; but the end of the regime at Yeltsin's hands was the revolution.

Gorbachev has to be counted as one of the great reformers in history.

Gorbachev undermined communism but failed to build a new system in its place.

The U.S.S.R. dissolved in 1991 into its component republics; Russia reemerged.

Identifications

500-Day plan	"union treaty"	Ukraine
Edward Shevardnadze	Committee of State	Belarus
Boris N. Yeltsin	Emergency	Commonwealth of Inde-
St. Petersburg	federation council	pendent States
the August coup		

Map Exercises

1. Can you locate the constituent republics of the Soviet Union before its dissolution? (See map, pp. 758–759, and tables, pp. 754 and 1016.)
2. Can you locate the independent states that have emerged? (See p. 1029 and maps, front and back end papers.)

127. After Communism

Study Questions

1. What problems were created by the revolutionary changes in central and eastern Europe in 1989? Why would the years that followed be a "period of painful transition"?
2. Discuss the major problems confronting (a) Russia after 1991, (b) the other former Soviet republics.
3. Why was it difficult for Yeltsin to cope with the economy? What kinds of economic programs did he try?
4. What led to Yeltsin's struggle with the legislature? What form did it take in 1993?
5. Discuss the emergence of nationalist tensions after the fall of communism. How did it manifest itself in Czechoslovakia?
6. Explain the background to the dissolution of Yugoslavia and the accompanying civil war. How was the conflict precipitated? What role did Serbia play in these events? the international community?
7. Discuss the economic, social, and political challenges confronting Western Europe in the 1990s. What challenges did Italy face? In what sense was Japan coping with problems similar to those of Western Europe?

Key Discussion Sentences

The revolutionary changes of 1989–1991 made possible but did not guarantee democratic and pluralist societies.

The new Russia, like the old Soviet Union, faced secessionist threats.

In domestic affairs Yeltsin was challenged by many of the same economic problems as Gorbachev.

The October Days of 1993 demonstrated that Russia was still living through a revolution.

Russia remained a great power.

Of all the explosive issues that confronted Europe after the downfall of communism, nationalism proved to be the most intractable.

When Yugoslavia's Communist reformers loosened the regime's authoritarian grip, separatist pressures exploded.

Western Europe faced a heavy burden of economic, social, and political troubles in the 1990s.

Immigration was changing the ethnic composition of the West European population.

The 1990s were an economic and political watershed for Japan also.

Identifications

Russian Federation	Duma	Christian Democrats
Georgia	pan-Serb ambitions	Popular party
Kazakhstan	Slobodan Milosevič	Forza Italia
Russian Congress of	"ethnic cleansing"	National Alliance
People's Deputies	Croatia	structural unem-
"economic shock	Slovenia	ployment
therapy"	Sarajevo	Japanese Liberal Demo-
October Days	Bosnia-Herzegovina	cratic Party

Map Exercises

1. Study the maps on pp. 470, 1034, and the front end papers. What may be said about the persistence of ethnic differences in central and eastern Europe? What have been some of the consequences since 1991?
2. By comparing the map on p. 1034 with that on the front end papers, explain the changes that have occurred in central and eastern Europe since 1991. What has happened to the Baltic republics? Czechoslovakia? Yugoslavia? What has accounted for the crisis in Bosnia?
3. Can you locate, using the maps on the front and back end papers, the republics of the former Soviet Union possessing nuclear missile bases in 1991?

128. Intellectual and Social Currents

Study Questions

1. What observations may be made about science, medicine, and public health in the contemporary era?
2. What may be said about twentieth-century advances in (a) nuclear physics, (b) the biological sciences?
3. Describe the problems for contemporary society created by (a) science, (b) technology. What major problems remain unresolved?
4. Assess the accomplishments and controversies relating to space exploration.
5. Discuss contemporary developments in (a) professional philosophy, (b) literary criticism, (c) the writing of history.
6. In what sense did modern art reflect a revolution against older traditions? How do the illustrations on pp. 584, 610, 633, 635, 780, 1051, and 1060 exemplify this revolution? What additional insights are added in pp. 970–971 of the Picture Essay?
7. What is meant by postmodernism? How does it differ from modernism?
8. What important developments may be noted in the major Western religions? What may be said about religious fundamentalism in the contemporary world? How has it manifested itself in Islam? In other religions?
9. In what sense was the activism of the 1960s a rebellion against modern society? Describe its outcome.
10. Discuss the accomplishments and continuing goals of the women's movement in contemporary society. Why might the movement have a different agenda in the developing world?

Key Discussion Sentences

Although contemporary culture had its origins in the years 1871–1914, it crossed new frontiers and took new directions in the course of the twentieth century.

Scientific discovery advanced more rapidly in the twentieth century than in all previous human history.

The transformation of physics in the twentieth century could be compared only to the scientific revolution of the sixteenth and seventeenth centuries.

Some questioned scientific and technological advances and asked whether modern technology had grown beyond human control.

The implications of genetic engineering were staggering.

Among the most dramatic technological achievements in the second half of the twentieth century was space exploration.

The existentialists grappled with the human predicament.

Much of modern or contemporary art prided itself on being nonobjective.

Postmodernism did not openly reject the commercialization and materialism of contemporary culture but embraced it and projected it in new ways.

The Roman Catholic church seemed to be in one of its important historic phases in the second half of the twentieth century.

Fundamentalism, especially in Islam, was on the rise.

The youth rebellion of the 1960s extended beyond the traditional generation gap.

The feminist, or women's liberation, movement was another manifestation of contemporary social ferment.

Identifications

Max Planck	Ludwig Wittgenstein	ecumenical movement
quantum physics	logical positivism	the Assumption
cyclotron	Jacques Derrida	John XXIII
Niels Bohr	deconstruction	*Pacem in Terris*
Enrico Fermi	*Annales* school	Vatican II
genetic code	*Learning from Las*	Paul VI
existentialism	*Vegas*	John Paul II
Jean-Paul Sartre	social gospel	"New Left"
		Simone de Beauvoir

129. A New Era

Study Questions

1. What dilemmas confronted United States policy makers in the years after the Cold War? the international community? What role could the United States be expected to play?
2. Discuss the dangers that nuclear arms continued to present. What progress was made on nuclear arms control? on nonproliferation?
3. Describe the shape of world affairs that seemed to be emerging in the 1990s. What role did Russia seem intent on playing?
4. How did the end of the Cold War open up new opportunities for the United Nations Security Council? What successes and what failures did it experience in these years?
5. What dilemmas for the international community did the disintegration of Yugoslavia create?
6. What problems did contemporary society face in connection with (a) population growth, (b) the environment, (c) the global economy, (d) relations between the industrial world and the developing world?

Key Discussion Sentences

The collapse of the Soviet Union transformed the foundations on which international relations had rested for over four decades.

The United States could not act as the world's policeman, but it could not easily abdicate its leadership role and responsibilities.

The end of the Cold War made it possible for the Security Council to return to the role originally intended for it.

The membership of the UN has grown dramatically in the years since 1945.

The explosion of virulent nationalism posed new challenges to the international community.

Nuclear nonproliferation remained high on the international agenda.

The time required to add a billion people to the world's population was growing strikingly shorter.

As grave a threat as the population explosion was, the planet faced environmental dangers as well.

The end of the Cold War did not bring peace to the world.

Identifications

Iraq	nuclear proliferation	population explosion
Kuwait	"checkbook di-	acid rain
Bosnia	plomacy"	Greens
North Korea	human rights	Amazon Forest

Map Exercises

1. Study the maps on the front and back end papers. Locate current and potential areas of friction and crisis mentioned in this chapter.
2. How do the tables on pp. 588 and 1063 demonstrate the world population explosion since about 1950? Using the maps on pp. 980–981 and the front and back end papers, show where most of the rapid growth has taken place. What do the insets in the latter maps tell you about population density?
3. Study the map, "Contemporary Europe," on the front end papers. On the outline map show the new states that have emerged since 1990 in central and eastern Europe, including the successor states in Europe of the former Soviet Union.

GENERAL ESSAY QUESTIONS FOR CHAPTER XXIV

1. Describe and compare the relationship between government and people in (a) Russia in the early twentieth century, (b) the Soviet Union, 1917–1991, and (c) Russia since 1991.

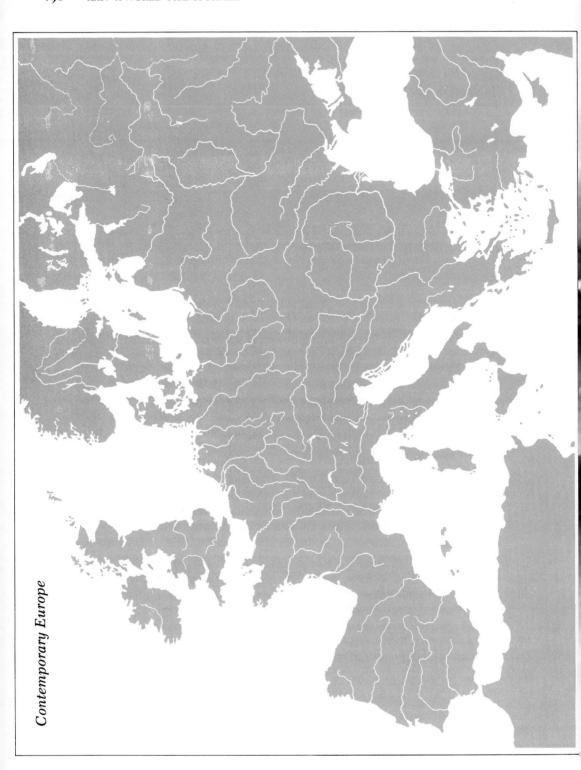

Contemporary Europe

2. Describe the experiences of the countries of central and eastern Europe (a) in the interwar years, (b) in the years 1945–1985, (c) in the years since 1985.
3. What brought about the collapse of communism (a) in central and eastern Europe, (b) in the U.S.S.R.? Was there a Revolution of 1989? of 1991?
4. What do historians mean by the "German question"? How was it revived by events in 1989? With what problems has the Federal Republic of Germany had to deal since reunification?
5. How would you compare the economic experiences of Western Europe in the years 1950 to 1974 and in the years since 1974? How successful has the effort been at economic and political integration?
6. How have contemporary movements in science, philosophy, religion, and the arts built upon the cultural and intellectual developments of the years 1871–1914? What new directions have emerged?
7. Describe the evolution of the United Nations since its inception. What have been its accomplishments and failures? What role have the developing nations played? What obstacles persist to the creation of a stronger UN?
8. What major challenges are likely to confront the world in the twenty-first century? On what theme would you in the 1990s conclude a history of the modern world?

GENERAL DISCUSSION PASSAGES FOR CHAPTER XXIV

The Cold War of the post-1945 years, brought on by Soviet ideology and expansionism, which in turn led to the American containment policy and countercrusade, ended. (p. 1017)

The revolutions of 1989–1991 reasserted ideals that were revolutionary when proclaimed in America in 1776, in France in 1789, throughout Europe in 1848, and in the West in 1919 and 1945. (p. 1011)

The prospects of a reunified Germany, possessing one of the world's most powerful economies, stirred grim ghosts of the past. (p. 1022)

It was difficult forty-five years after the end of the Second World to deny the German people the right to self-determination, and it was unreasonable to insist upon unalterable traits of national character, or blame the Nazi atrocities on the generations that followed. (p. 1022)

Marginal as socialism was in American life, democratic socialism still had a lingering appeal in Europe. (p. 1031)

Marxism, born in the nineteenth century in response to the instability and inequities of capitalism, could survive as a scholarly and analytical tool, but it seemed destined to limited appeal as a political philosophy, at least in the distorted form given it by Lenin and the Russian Revolution of 1917. (p. 1030)

The revolutionary changes of 1989–1991 also released many ugly currents, ominous for the future. (p. 1030)

Countries already possessing capitalist market economies and democratic political systems were also challenged to create societies that would overcome economic instability, insecurity, unemployment, and social injustices. (p. 1031)

Science has always affected the way people have thought about themselves and their universe. This was true of the Copernican revolution, Darwinian evolution, and twentieth-century physics. (p. 1044)

Some questioned scientific and technological advance and asked whether modern technology had grown beyond human control. (p. 1044)

The advance of science and technology was no longer equated with the idea of progress. (p. 1045)

The world had to live with nuclear arms; the genie could not be put back into the bottle. (p. 1058)

The techniques developed to save or prolong human life raised ethical and legal issues, including new definitions of life and death. (pp. 1044–1045)

Existentialism emphasized the anguish of human existence, the frailty of human reason, the fragility of human institutions, and the need to reassert and redefine human freedom. (p. 1047)

Contemporary art seemed to mirror the political turbulence of the times and the disillusionment with rationalism and optimism. (p. 1048)

Although there were disagreements in and outside the women's liberation movement on the methods and tempo of change, wide agreement existed on the need to utilize fully all of society's human resources in every part of the globe. If that could be accomplished, it would count among the most memorable of the revolutionary changes of the contemporary era. (p. 1057)

Religious fundamentalism ran counter to the blending of cultures in the contemporary world. (p. 1054)

Human rights, no matter how difficult to define, whether of Western origin or not, represented a common core of values. (p. 1062)

The world was still fumbling its way toward an international community of sovereign states, unsure of how to secure peace, security, and justice for the world's peoples. (p. 1062)

A cataclysm is not a time of downfall only. Mountains crumble, but others are thrust up. Lands vanish, but others rise from the sea. So it is with the political and social cataclysm of our times. (p. 1065)

To close this long history on a note of placidity would indeed be inappropriate, but so, too, would it be to close it on a note of doom. (p. 1065)

ABOUT THE AUTHORS

R. R. PALMER was born in Chicago. After graduating from the University of Chicago he received his doctorate from Cornell University in 1934. From 1936 to 1963 he taught at Princeton University, was then at Washington University in St. Louis from 1963 to 1966, and at Yale from 1969 until his retirement in 1977. He now resides in Princeton, where he is affiliated with the Institute for Advanced Study. His books include *Twelve Who Ruled: The Year of the Terror in the French Revolution* (1941, 1989), and the two-volume *Age of the Democratic Revolution* (1959 and 1964), both volumes of which were History Book Club selections, and the first of which won the Bancroft Prize in 1960. He has likewise written *The World of the French Revolution* (1970) and *The Improvement of Humanity: Education and the French Revolution* (1985), and has edited the *Rand McNally Atlas of World History* (1957). He is the translator of Georges Lefebvre's *Coming of the French Revolution* (1947, 1989), Louis Bergeron's *France under Napoleon* (1981), and Jean-Paul Bertaud's *Army of the French Revolution: From Citizen-Soldiers to Instrument of Power* (1988), and editor-translator of *From Jacobin to Liberal: Marc-Antoine Jullien, 1775–1848* (1993). He was president of the American Historical Association in 1970. He has received honorary degrees from the Universities of Uppsala and Toulouse, and was awarded the Antonio Feltrinelli International Prize for History at Rome in 1990.

JOEL COLTON was born in New York City. He graduated from the City College of New York, served as a military intelligence officer in Europe in World War II, and received his Ph.D. from Columbia University in 1950. He joined the Department of History at Duke University in 1947, chaired the department from 1967 to 1974, received a Distinguished Teaching Award in 1986, and became emeritus professor in 1989. From 1974 to 1981, on leave from Duke University, he served with the Rockefeller Foundation in New York as director of its research and fellowship program in the humanities. In 1979 he was elected a Fellow of the American Academy of Arts and Sciences and was named a national Phi Beta Kappa lecturer in 1983–1984. He has received Guggenheim, Rockefeller Foundation, and National Endowment for the Humanities fellowships. He has served on the editorial board of the *Journal of Modern History* and of *French Historical Studies,* and on the advisory board of *Historical Abstracts.* He has been vice-president of the Society of French Historical Studies and co-president of the International Commission on the History of Social Movements and Social Structures. His writings include *Compulsory Labor Arbitration in France, 1936–1939* (1951); *Léon Blum: Humanist in Politics* (1966, 1987), for which he received a Mayflower Award; *Twentieth Century* (1968, 1980), in the *Time-Life Great Ages of Man* series; and numerous contributions to journals, encyclopedias, and collaborative volumes.

ILLUSTRATION SOURCES